THE COLLECTED STORIES OF
WOLFGANG HILDESHEIMER

THE
COLLECTED
STORIES
OF
WOLFGANG
HILDESHEIMER

TRANSLATED BY
JOACHIM NEUGROSCHEL

THE ECCO PRESS
NEW YORK

First published in 1987 by The Ecco Press
18 West 30th Street, New York, N.Y. 10001
Published simultaneously in Canada by
Penguin Books Canada Ltd., Ontario
Printed in the United States of America

Designed by Francesca Belanger

"The Vacation" first appeared in *Antaeus*.

Publication of this book was made possible in part by a grant
from the National Endowment for the Arts.

Library of Congress Cataloging in Publication Data
Hildesheimer, Wolfgang. 1916–
    The collected stories of Wolfgang Hildesheimer.
    1. Hildesheimer, Wolfgang, 1916–   —Translations,
English.   I. Title.
PT2617.I354A25   1987   833′.914   87-456
ISBN 0-88001-131-9
ISBN 0-88001-132-7 (pbk.)

CONTENTS

CONTENTS

THE COLLECTED STORIES OF
WOLFGANG HILDESHEIMER

THE END

OF A WORLD

The final soiree given by the Marchesa Monte-tristo made a lasting impact on me. Its impact was, of course, heightened by the strange, almost unique, conclusion. This alone was an event not easily forgotten. It was truly a memorable evening.

My acquaintanceship with the marchesa (née Waterman, from Little Gidding, Ohio) was a matter of sheer chance. Through the good offices of my friend Herr von Perlhuhn (the Abraham a Sancta Clara scholar, *not* the neomystic), I had sold her the bathtub in which Marat was assassinated, and which (as may not be generally known) had been in my possession until the sale. Gambling debts had forced me to dispose of several pieces in my collection. That was how I came to the marchesa, who had long been hunting this item for her collection of washing utensils of the eighteenth century.

We met for tea, agreeing on a price after a brief, cordial

negotiation. Our chat then touched upon topics of interest to many collectors and connoisseurs. I noticed that the ownership of that rare item gained me a certain prestige in her eyes, and I was therefore not surprised the day she invited me to one of her renowned soirees at her palazzo on the artificial island of San Amerigo.

The island had been created for the marchesa several kilometers southeast of Murano. She had yielded to sudden inspiration, for she despised the mainland (she said it was injurious to her mental equilibrium), but had been unable to choose from the available selection of islands, especially because she could not endure the thought of having to share one with somebody else. Now she resided here, devoting her life to preserving the tried and true and awakening the forgotten, or, as she preferred to put it, cultivating things genuine and lasting.

The invitation said that the soiree was scheduled for eight P.M., but the guests were not expected before ten. Furthermore, custom demanded that we go there in gondolas. The crossing thus took almost two hours, and was difficult if not dangerous on a rough sea (indeed, some previous guests had failed to reach their destination, finding, instead, a seaman's grave); but only a barbarian would have flouted these unwritten rules of style, and barbarians were never invited. Any candidate whose general deportment hinted at even the slightest qualm about the possible treachery of such a voyage would never have been included in the guest list. Needless to say, the marchesa was not mistaken about me—even though I may have become a failure in her eyes at the end of the evening.

However, she survived her disappointment by only a few minutes, and that comforts me.

The splendor of the palazzo is something I need not describe, for on the outside it was an exact replica of the Palazzo Vendramin, and on the inside all stylistic eras, starting with the Gothic, were represented, but, naturally, not interwoven; each era had its own room; the marchesa could never be accused of aesthetic incongruities. Nor shall I mention her luxurious hospitality; anyone who has ever been to a state banquet in a monarchy—and that is the kind of function I mainly attend—will know what the evening was like. Furthermore, we would not be honoring the wishes of the marchesa and her circle by indulging in voluptuous memories of culinary delights, especially here, where my aim is to describe the final hours of several illustrious minds of our century, which demise I had the good fortune to witness as sole survivor—a fluke that, however, imposes a certain responsibility on me.

After exchanging cordialities with the hostess and fondling her pack of long-haired Pekingese, which never left her side, I was introduced to Madame Dombrowska, one of the truly great double talents of our time. First of all, Dombrowska must be credited with actually renewing rhythmical expressive dance, a genre that became a mystical action under her feet, but that, unfortunately, as good as perished with her (may I recall Basiliewsky's bon mot: "There is no dance, there are only dancers!"). Furthermore, Dombrowska was also the author of the book *Back to Youth*, which, as the title states, advocates a return to Jugendstil and has meanwhile—I scarcely need mention it—made a great stir in wide circles.

As we were chatting, a tall, elderly gentleman came toward us. I instantly recognized him by his profile: it was Golch. *The* Golch. (Everyone knows who he is: his intellectual contributions have become a delightful part of our heritage.) Dombrowska introduced me: "Herr Sebald, the former owner of Marat's bathtub." Word had gotten abroad.

"Aha," said Golch, executing a light upward glissando on the last syllable of his exclamation, thereby implying that he might consider me a pretender for the elite of culture bearers, although I would still have to pass any number of tests. I instantly seized the opportunity to ask him whether he had liked the exhibition of contemporary painting at the Luxembourg. Gazing up, as if seeking a word in space, Golch said: "Passé!" (He employed the then common British pronunciation of the word. The words *cliché* and *pastiche* were likewise stressed in the British way. I do not know how they are pronounced now, nor does it strike me as important. After all, the island of the marchesa was style-setting in such matters. The island sank, taking along its guidelines. "Passé," he said, and I agreed, and would have done so—I must confess!— even had he expressed the opposite opinion, for, after all, it *was* Golch I was conversing with.

The guests now went to the buffet. Here, I bumped into Signora Sgambati, the astrologer, who had created quite a sensation some time ago with her theory that the stars revealed not only individual destinies but also whole currents in cultural history. True, the current predicted by her had not yet set in, but, as her large following maintained, little eddies were forming here and there, vortices that could be viewed as symptomatic cells. She was no run-of-the-mill person, that Sgambati—you could tell just by looking at her. Nevertheless, under the circumstances, I find it incomprehensible that the constellation had failed to inform her of the imminent deaths of some of the seminal members of the intellectual world, the very creators of her current. She was absorbed in a conversation with Professor Kuntz-Sartori, the politician and advocate of royalist ideas, who had been trying for decades to introduce a monarchy into Switzerland, whereby, to be sure, he met with considerable resistance from the Helvetian Confederation. An outstanding mind!

After partaking of refreshment in the form of champagne and delicious crustaceans, the guests entered the Silver Room. For now came the high point of the evening, a very special performance: the premiere of two flute sonatas by Antonio Giambattista Bloch, a contemporary and friend of Rameau, discovered by the musicologist Weldli, who was also present at the soiree, of course. The pieces were played by the flautist Bérenger (yes indeed, a descendant) and accompanied by the marchesa herself, on the harpsichord at which Célestine Rameau had taught her son the fundamentals of counterpoint (to be sure, he never properly understood them till his dying day), and which had been transported here from Paris. The flute too had its history, but I have forgotten it. The two interpreters had donned Rococo garb for the occasion, and the small ensemble, having deliberately arranged itself to this end, resembled a Watteau painting. Needless to say, the performance took place in muted candlelight. There was no one present who would not have found electric light unendurable for such an occasion. Consistent with another tactful whim of the marchesa's, the audience, after hearing the first sonata (D major), had to move from the Silver Room (Baroque) to the Gold Room (Early Rococo) in order to hear the second sonata (F minor). For the first room had a major timbre, but this one was minor—a point that no one would have challenged.

I must, however, say that the bleak elegance inherent in flute sonatas of second-rate and especially newly discovered maestros of that period is explained in this case by the fact that Antonio Giambattista Bloch never existed; the works performed were penned by the scholar Weltli. Although this did not come out until much later, I cannot help retrospectively viewing it as a bit degrading for the marchesa that she spent her final minutes performing (albeit brilliantly) a forgery.

During the second movement of the F Minor Sonata, I saw a rat scurry along the wall. I was amazed. At first, I thought it had been lured by the flute playing, for rats, as we know, are very musical, but it was scurrying in the opposite direction, that is, fleeing the music. It was followed by a second rat. I looked at the other guests. They had not noticed anything, especially since most of them had shut their eyes in order to abandon themselves in blissful relaxation to the sounds of Weltli's counterfeit. Now, I heard a dull rumble, like a clap of very distant thunder. The floor vibrated. Again I looked at the guests. If they did hear anything (and they must have caught something), it could not be inferred from their poses of almost formless absorption. I, however, was disquieted by these odd symptoms.

A footman entered quietly. The stylish, snugly laced livery worn by the marchesa's entire personnel made him look like a supernumerary in *Tosca*—but that is neither here nor there. Tiptoeing over to the performers, he whispered something to the marchesa. I saw her turn pale—it looked quite becoming in the dim candlelight, and one might almost have taken it for a lovingly planned part of the ceremony—but she pulled herself together and calmly completed the andante without interrupting; she almost seemed to draw out the final fermata. Then she signaled to the flautist, stood up, and addressed the listeners.

"My honored guests," she said, "I have just learned that the foundations of the island, and with them those of the palazzo, are disintegrating. The maritime civil engineering corps has been notified. However, I feel I am speaking for all of us when I say that we will continue with the music." Her dignified words were rewarded with silent gestures of assent.

She sat down again, signaled to Monsieur Bérenger, and they played the allegro con brio, the final movement, which, although I did not realize they were performing a forgery, struck me as doing little justice to the uniqueness of the situation.

Small puddles emerged on the parquet. The rumbling had intensified and sounded closer. Most of the guests had straightened up by now and, with their faces ashen in the candlelight, they sat as if patiently awaiting a sculptor who would immortalize them in poses of final, euphoric aplomb for an admiring posterity.

I, however, stood up and said, "I'm leaving," softly enough not to offend the musicians, but loud enough to let the other guests know that I was courageous enough to acknowledge my sudden feeling of distance. By now, the floor was almost entirely covered with water. Even though I left on tiptoe, my feet got wet, and I could not avoid splashing a few evening gowns as I cautiously wended my way out. But this damage was slight, after all, considering what was about to happen. Few of the guests so much as deigned to glance at me from barely raised lids, but this made no difference to me, I no longer belonged. When I opened the French door, a wave flooded into the room, causing Lady Fitzwilliam (the custodian of the Celtic heritage) to pull her fur coat more snugly around her shoulders—a reflex action, no doubt, for it was not very useful. Before closing the door behind me, I saw Herr von Perlhuhn (the neomystic, *not* the Abraham a Sancta Clara scholar) glancing at me, half-scornfully, half-dismally, as if he had assumed the painful task of transmitting the general disappointment. He was almost up to his knees in water, like the marchesa, who was no longer able to use the pedals. Now I do not know whether they are very important on a harpsichord. I thought to myself that had the piece been a cello sonata, they would have been forced to break off, since the instrument's body yields little or no resonance in water. It is odd what inappropriate thoughts one often has at such moments.

The vestibule was suddenly as silent as a grotto. The only sounds were a distant roaring intensified by occasional echoes. I stripped off my tuxedo jacket and swam with powerful chest strokes through the sinking palace, toward the gates. The waves I created thudded softly against the walls and columns. The area sounded like an indoor swimming pool. One is seldom granted a chance to exercise in such a framework. No one was to be seen. The domestics had evidently fled. And why not? They had no obligation to true and genuine culture, and the people gathered here no longer required their services. Outside, a clear, calm moon was shining, as if nothing were happening; and yet a world (in the true sense of the term) was sinking here. As if from very far away, I could still hear Monsieur Bérenger's higher flute trills. He lipped well, there's no denying it.

I untied the last gondola, which the fleeing staff had left, and I put out to sea. As I rowed past the windows, the waves poured into the palace, making the curtains belly like wet sails. I saw that the guests had risen from their seats. The sonata must have ended, for they were applauding, for which purpose they held their hands over their heads, the water being up to their chins. The marchesa and Monsieur Bérenger accepted the applause with dignity. Under the circumstances, however, they could not take bows.

Now, the water reached the candles. They slowly went out, and silence came with increasing darkness; the applause faded and stopped, as if at a terrible signal. Suddenly, the roar of a collapsing building commenced. The palazzo fell. I steered the gondola seaward to keep from being hit by falling stucco. It is very difficult brushing it out of one's clothes after the dust has settled in.

Having rowed several hundred yards through the lagoon, toward the Island of San Giorgio, I looked back once more. The sea lay smooth, like a mirror in the moonlight, as if no island had ever been there.

Too bad about the tub, I thought, for this loss could not be made good. My thought may have been hard-hearted; but, as experience teaches, one needs a certain detachment to grasp the full scope of such an occurrence.

I AM NOT WRITING

A BOOK ON

KAFKA

Evil tongues, or rather their owners, claim (and I can see them sneering) that I am writing a book on Kafka. This accusation is false, I repudiate it. For I am working on a book on Golch.

To be perfectly honest, I would like to admit that a long time ago I did toy with the idea—as every sensitive intellectual does—of writing a book on Kafka. One has to go through this stage, and subsequently one need not feel any more embarrassed about it than about any juvenile crush. However, the thing that kept me from carrying it out was not so much a shift of interest as the circumstance that all the people I knew were already working on a book about Kafka (not all of them on one book, but each on his own, of course). Through some whim of destiny, that I truly have no reason to regret, they had all begun their project early (I am a relatively late bloomer); and now, there was no aspect left in light of which I might have interpreted Kafka. That was why

I briefly toyed with the idea of selecting one of the more important Kafka biographers and writing a book on him; but even this idea was anticipated by someone else, who, like me, had been tardy in coming to the distribution of aspects.

I now resolved to seek a new field, and I found one. I am working, as I have said, on a book about Ekkehard Golch. For those unfamiliar with this name—and there are all too many people in that situation—I would like to offer a rough sketch of his personality.

Aside from an equally eventless youth, Golch, who died in 1929 at the age of eighty-six, spent his entire life as a schoolteacher in Altzmünzach, a town in which express trains do not stop. It is due less to this fact than to his indifference toward the realm of variety that he never left Almünzach, devoting his life with tireless concentration to his work. (My chapter "Inner Travels" deals with those trains of thought, on a level that would go beyond the parameters of this brief apologia.)

Golch taught English and German at the High School for Daughters (this institution actually existed then and still does today). After a few analytical efforts, of which the essay "Körner's Female Characters" is probably the strongest (unfortunately, it would scarcely be noticed today because of its historical limitations), he dedicated himself to his opus magnum, on the life and work of James Boswell, the important biographer of Dr. Johnson, the immortal British lexicographer. Not only is this a work of major psychological intensity and enormous conviction, but, being nine volumes long, it exceeds in quantity the life's work of both Boswell *and* Johnson.

I do not wish to give away my book at this point; still (and the reader will find the self-assurance I reveal here justified), I would like to emphasize not only that my work, which already exists in manuscript form (except for the concluding chapter, "On the Nature of Biography"), has managed compellingly to depict my hero's powerful Boswell experience, but also that I have done the reverse, namely, illuminated Boswell in Golch's light, whereby I have in turn seen the self-willed Dr. Johnson through Boswell's spectacles (metaphorically; Boswell did not wear glasses), as he, interpreted by Golch, appears to me: to some extent, a triple dissolve of Dr. Johnson's "core personality" (in this sense, my neologism; it has nothing to do with the Jungian school).

My book is good, there can be no doubt. It fills a gap. I would venture to maintain that my solid connoisseurship and my ability to project myself into the mentality of kindred spirits, both virtues being revealed in this book, will some day move a biographer to devote at least a detailed necrologue to me in my quality as the biographer of Golch. And as for the claim that I am writing a book on Kafka, it will be refuted with the publication of my work. For even the owners of evil tongues must realize that one cannot write about Kafka *and* about Golch.

1 9 5 6—

A PILZ YEAR

T he year 1956 is almost over, and with it fades the memory of many immortals, whose birthdays and death days have been commemorated during several months of festivals and festivities: Mozart, Heine, Rembrandt, Caesar, and Freud—ceremonial speakers, wreath layers, heads of state, and the diplomatic corps have barely had a moment to themselves. But one man has been forgotten: Gottlieb Theodor Pilz, who died one hundred years ago, on September 12, 1856. His significance is still underestimated today. This is not surprising. For he was not so much a creator as a damper. His contribution to the history of Western civilization was expressed in the nonexistence of works which never came into being thanks to his courageous, self-sacrificing interference. No wonder posterity, which is accustomed to assessing great minds in terms of their creativity and not their omissions, remembers him seldom if ever.

Gottlieb Theodor Pilz was born in 1789 as the son of

well-to-do Protestant parents in Dinkelsbühl or Nördlingen, Germany. The controversy about his true place of birth has never been properly settled; hence, both towns exhibit his birth house. (Cf. G. S. Grützbacher, "Is Pilz a Dinkelsbühler? Contributions to a Moot Point," *The Journal of Applied Culture*, vol. XXII [1881].) The impressions of his youth made a vital contribution to Gottlieb Theodor's development.[1] His mother sang chorales by Buxtehude for the infant in his cradle; and no sooner had he outgrown them than his father read him Tacitus and Milton in his own translations.

In 1798, the family moved to Hamburg, where the nine-year-old boy encountered the intellectual life of the period. One of the regular guests in the Pilz house was the German poet Klopstock, who would read aloud from his *Messiah* or even his odes, of which he penned several hundred every month despite his advanced age. In a letter to Meyerbeer in 1836, Pilz describes these readings, during which he filched whole piles of odes from the already rather myopic poet, who never even noticed the loss. (Cf. *The Seven Letters of Gottlieb Theodor Pilz*, ed. Karl Ferdinand Gutzkow [Cottasche Verlagsbuchhandlung, 1864].)

The poets of Storm and Stress also frequented the Pilz home, spreading the wind of Unconditional Rebellion and introducing the notion of Freedom. Plus the National Indignation, and the sense of Humiliation, which was on the agenda back then. Young Gottlieb Theodor, swept up by the vague whirlwind of sedition, reached for his quill and, in the creative delirium of a tempestuous night, penned his first and

15

only drama: *Duke Theodore of Gothland.* It was the year 1804; Pilz was fifteen.

After graduating from secondary school, Pilz traveled to Italy, remaining there until 1809. During this period, the adolescent revealed the characteristic traits that made him the person we honor today: throughout his southern sojourn, which lasted two years, he never kept a diary. Neither taking notes nor making sketches, he never set down in any form his thoughts on Italian culture. Not a single utterance of his has come down to us; indeed, upon viewing the Gulf of Naples, he supposedly did not bat an eyelash. In the year 1808, he wrote one letter.[2] This letter is characterized by a refreshing sobriety that was truly rare in that era, which is why it is quoted here:

> Palermo, Casa Gozzoli
> 7th of October, 1808

> Dearest Mother,
>   It is very nice here, and I therefore plan to remain a While. I would be grateful to You if You could be so kind as to send me my velvet Jabot, since the Evenings here are cool.
>   With my very fondest Wishes I remain

>   Your loving Son,
>   Gottlieb Theodor

Pilz spent a long period in Rome, as we learn from jottings by August Wilhelm von Schlegel, who, together with Madame de Staël, encountered him there in the year 1808. Schlegel

writes that they ran into him on Via Appia, where Pilz was
sitting in the sun (Pilz may be credited with being the pioneer
of sitting in the sun), and Schlegel asked him how to get to
the Caracalla Baths, the goal of their promenade. Pilz replied
that he was a stranger here himself. Having thus established
the common ground of their situation, they began to converse.
Pilz, however (according to Schlegel), was "rather impolite,"
scarcely looking at the two of them and constantly squinting
at the sun. In reality, as he later explained, he was "enraged
at the Disturbance and the bustling Zealousness of that Staël
Woman"; he became nervous and monosyllabic, and when
Madame de Staël, without being asked, volunteered the information that she was planning to write a book on Germany,
Pilz gruffly asked:

"What for?"

Madame de Staël had never thought about this and she
failed to come up with an answer.

They met several times at the Café Greco. Sipping a double
cappuccino, Pilz tried to talk Madame de Staël out of going
ahead with her plan. But it was useless: she refused to give
up her idea of documenting her love for Germany. The four-
volume opus, *De l'Allemagne,* appeared in 1813.

In 1810, Pilz was in Berlin, where by sheer chance he met
Friedrich Ludwig Jahn. This patriot warmed up to the twenty-
one-year-old (the nature of these affinities has, unfortunately,
not come down to us) and told him about his plans: he wanted
to pen a vast allegorical cycle depicting the freedom struggle
of the ancient Teutons against the Roman tyranny. Having
already written down a few scenes about the preparations for

the Battle of the Teutoburg Forest, he wanted to read them to Pilz. Not only did Pilz emphatically refuse, but he took this opportunity to have a heart-to-heart talk with the older man. He told him that he, Jahn, was on the wrong track. There had been and would still be enough Teutoburg Forest battles. (Prophetic words!) No, Pilz argued, without his wishing to belittle the measure of Jahn's intellectual gifts in any way, his true abilities might be realized in some other area—indeed, did he not have a secret propensity for physical exercises? Why not, said Pilz, turn this propensity into a sublime calling and devote his life to strengthening German youth with physical discipline by showing it how to exercise? Perhaps he should even call himself Turnvater Jahn (Gym-Father Jahn), a name that would instantly give him a certain lasting aura! Jahn was instantly enflamed by this—really extraordinary— idea; he ripped up the manuscript of his Teutoburg Battle and, so far as is known, he never again worked on a theatrical drama. The first gymnastics arena was built for him in 1811.

Pilz's whereabouts during the next three years are still unknown. In 1814, we meet him in Vienna, attending the premiere of the revised *Fidelio.* Nothing is known about the impression that this opera made on the twenty-five-year-old. Presumably, he said nothing about it. But we do know that during his Viennese period he saw a great deal of Beethoven, and the master's dry spell, which, as we know, lasted from 1814 to 1818, may have been caused by these meetings; but this is merely a thesis, requiring documentation by future scholars.

Pilz's second letter was written in 1815. It was addressed

to his father. In this letter, he writes that he has succeeded in talking Mühlwesel[3] out of his plan to write an opera trilogy about the Hapsburg dynasty; Pilz did so by introducing the composer to the pleasures of tarot. "M. was at first stubborn, claiming he was a Musician, not an Idler, and anything that Beethoven could do, Mühlwesel could do too. That might be, I replied, but that was no Reason to actually carry out his Plan. Where would we be, I said, if we wanted to do everything that someone else was able to do! He finally gave in. I myself intend to spend a few Weeks in Switzerland recovering from my recent Stress and Strains."

Several weeks became several years. Madame de Staël saw him in 1819; he was lying in the sun on the banks of Lake Geneva, near her country estate. He did not react when she called to him. Presumably, he pretended to be asleep, for there was nothing about her company that tempted him. In this way, Pilz again distinguished himself from countless men of his era.

In 1821, Pilz returned to Berlin, where he met people like E. T. A. Hoffmann. One evening, Hoffmann talked Pilz into joining him and Ludwig Devrient to carouse at Luther's and Wegener's taverns. Having always been anything but averse to wine, Pilz saw an opportunity to show his drama to the theater man Devrient. But he never got the chance. For there was a young man at the next table, "behaving quite horribly in his deep Drunkenness." Pilz learned that this was a student named Grabbe (Christian Dietrich), who styled himself a poet and felt it was his mission to drive Shakespeare off the German stage.

Gottlieb Theodor's interest was aroused. He walked over to the young man, who promptly overwhelmed him with bawdy babbling, in which Pilz soon discerned this queer bird's *idée fixe:* Shakespeare was supposedly a hack and couldn't do much better than scrawl opera libretti. Pilz rightly felt it made no sense getting involved in this conversation; instead, he tried to calm him down by toasting him. But Grabbe dug in his heels and, in order to lend strength to his almost incomprehensible words, pulled out a manuscript, which he tossed over to Pilz: his libretto based on Shakespeare's *The Merry Wives of Windsor.* Pilz pocketed it, and when Grabbe asked for it back, Pilz, no longer sober himself, tossed over his *Duke Theodore of Gothland,* which Grabbe pocketed.

Grabbe never noticed the accidental exchange. This drama is still considered a magnum opus of this German poet. But the true author was Pilz.

From 1823 to 1840, Pilz lived in Paris. In 1824, he made the acquaintance of Baroness Aurore Dupin-Dudevant. She instantly felt a tender affection for the thirty-five-year-old. Pilz, however, did not care to get involved; he advised the— exceedingly intelligent—woman to wear men's clothing, call herself George Sand, and write novels, which she did. Granted, this action was strangely disharmonious with his creativity, and some critics have pilloried it as thoughtless, nay, irresponsible. The fact is that Pilz, inspired by the urgent —and understandable—wish to divert the baroness's attention from him, never seriously believed she would follow his advice. By the time he realized his error and presented Cho-

pin to her, it was too late; that is, she remained with Chopin
and literature.

Incidentally (and this is not generally known), it was Pilz
who in 1835 persuaded Chopin not to wear women's clothing
and call himself Aurore Dupin. This action likewise brought
Pilz some harsh criticism, although in this case, his support-
ers, who would not miss mazurkas, études, and waltzes, are
in the majority.

In 1828, while attending the Opéra with George Sand, Pilz
made the acquaintance of Meyerbeer, and the two men soon
became friends. At their very first meeting, Pilz tried to make
Meyerbeer realize that he had missed his calling. But Meyerbeer could not be talked out of it. He claimed that a similar
success would not be his in any other field, and that he was
giving the public what it wanted to see and hear. Pilz soon
realized the futility of his efforts, and one evening he showed
him Grabbe's *Merry Wives of Windsor:* Would Meyerbeer
care to set it to music? After thoroughly studying the manuscript, the composer refused, explaining that the libretto
did not offer enough possibilities for spectacle and show-
manship.

Pilz then decided to send the libretto to Beethoven, and he
wrote his third letter (dated November 22, 1828). "Incidentally," he said, "I recently heard your Fifth Symphony. Not
bad, not bad at all! Nevertheless, dear maestro, it is my
opinion that you ought to focus on cheerier things and take
a vacation from the titanic. For once, forget your tragic existence, especially since it must be highly strenuous! How about
an opera based on *The Merry Wives of Windsor*? The libretto

is finished!" The letter was returned, for Beethoven had died in 1827.

Pilz had no more success when he showed Grabbe's libretto to Berlioz; and so, after taking some lessons in music theory, he composed the opera himself in 1837, using the pseudonym Otto Nicolai.

In 1836, Gottlieb Theodor Pilz was at the height of his powers. This was not only the year in which, after a hard struggle, he managed to talk Delacroix out of painting a series of colossal pictures of various jungle scenes, but he also wrote two letters. Both of them were addressed to Meyerbeer, who was sojourning in Berlin. The first letter is more reflective in nature. It bears witness to its author's immaculate self-criticism in that it deals with the development of his artistic and receptive conscience, which he describes as the cause and motive force of his delaying effect. Between the lines, we again find a timid attempt to talk the composer out of constantly writing operas. (Meyerbeer, whose most outstanding feature was his true generosity, never resented these efforts.)

The second letter is extremely informative, depicting, as it does, Gottlieb Theodor's tireless endeavors in the area of dampening. We may quote the following paragraph.

"In the evening, at Rossini's. The meal was excellent, as always. Among other delicious dishes, he served a tournedo, which, as Alfred [i.e., De Musset] said, would alone suffice to establish Rossini's immortality. I took up this grand idea and tried to talk Rossini into devoting himself exclusively to gastronomy. He said he would think about it."

These repeated efforts were finally crowned with success. The Tournedo à la Rossini (1838) contributed to the maestro's fame at least as much as his *Stabat Mater,* which he penned six years later; this was his last achievement in the area of music. From then on, until his death in 1868, he never wrote another note or touched an instrument; he concentrated entirely on gourmet cooking, which owes him several lasting creations.

Pilz's next letter, written in 1841, was to his laundress and is therefore less revealing. He talks about several silk cravats that have gone astray. The Cotta edition includes this letter only for the sake of thoroughness.

During these years, Pilz was elected to the jury of the Académie des Beaux Arts, in which office he advocating drawing lots to determine the acceptance or rejection of submitted works, since, as he pointed out, their value made it quite indifferent which were shown and which refused. This suggestion was not followed; quite the contrary: it brought Pilz the hatred of several important painters, who are slumbering in utter oblivion today, thus posthumously justifying Gottlieb Theodor's proposal.

Otherwise, few details are known about his creativity during these years. But we may assume that he fought indefatigably against the artistic overexuberance of the times; it is largely owing to him that the number of works produced in that era did not become more rampant. Still, it would be wrong to blame his existence for the brief lives of several potentially significant Romantic masters, as so many late-nineteenth-century critics felt called upon to do. We can only cry to them: The art of your era would not have suffered from a damper of Pilz's format!

Pilz spent the years 1842 to 1850 traveling through Italy, Switzerland, and Germany, where he met Schumann and Mendelssohn, to whom he successfully presented his theory that a composer should not write more than four symphonies. He never put this theory to paper; its gist is, therefore, not known, alas, and we must even fear that it was not meant seriously. Nevertheless, these two Romantic masters did go along with it. Each limited his number of symphonies to four, and Schubert even successfully influenced Brahms in this direction.

The year 1849 brought Gottlieb Theodor's last letter. Written in Munich, it was addressed to George Sand. This missive may be viewed as the conclusion and summing-up of Pilz's work, and it might be the letter that touches us most deeply today, not only because of the maxim coined therein, "More words, fewer deeds!" (what thinking person would not truly wish that this maxim had gained greater validity?), but chiefly because of the modest, resigned manner in which Pilz reviews his successes and failures, describing his life as not influential enough to struggle against the enormous creative urge of his era. Between the lines, we can glean his disappointment at not leaving behind any disciples to carry on his work. Today, one still reads his letter with sympathy, perhaps even a touch of poignancy.

In 1852, Pilz returned to Paris, spending his last years visiting various great men, who were kept from their creative work by his witty conversations. His own salon gained an almost legendary prestige.

He was struck down by a dramatic death on September 12, 1856, at one of his soirees. He had spent his final days abridging Racine's tragedies into a single one-act play, thus hoping to preserve this poet's impact for several more decades. Pilz was reciting Phaedra's great monologue from this version. Suddenly, he collapsed on the floor, lifeless. The onlookers applauded. They thought that this gesture had crowned the recital. Only gradually did the audience, deeply shaken, realize that the sixty-seven-year-old had passed away. The German physician, who hurried over too late, diagnosed the cause of death as a stroke resulting from a neglected case of prickly heat.

Gottlieb Theodor Pilz has found many critics who never tire of attacking his inhibiting effect on the organic development of Romanticism. Admittedly, since the nonexistence of the works prevented by him will, of course, make any judgment of them impossible, certain works rejected in advance by him might have been preserved down to our own era. Nevertheless, his efforts had a beneficial, nay, liberating impact on all areas of art. How much have we been spared thanks to him, the great and unique man! He passed on prematurely, and we cannot help stating that a Pilz would be useful today too.

In response to his express wish, uttered shortly before his death, no monuments have been put up to Gottlieb Theodor Pilz; instead, his entire estate was turned over to easily enthused, but untalented young men, in exchange for the promise that they would never do any creative work again. Unfortunately, this possibility was exhausted long since; and thus, the spirit of Gottlieb Theodor has died out.

As a result, there were very few knowledgeable people who attended the simple celebration at the graveside of this important man on the centennial of his death.

Notes

1. As Gustav Prossnik emphasizes in his (incidentally, extremely valuable!) study *The Youth of Great Men,* this is probably the only way in which Pilz is not so very different from other great men.

2. Unfortunately, the original manuscripts of these seven missives were lost in the Great Fire of Hamburg. Recently, the editor, Karl Ferdinand Gutzkow, has drawn hostile criticism because of the rather arbitrary approach of his versions of Büchner. However, there is no reason whatsoever to assume that he altered Pilz's letters in any way, shape, or form.

3. Franz Xaver Mühlwesel, 1778–1859, a zither player of stature, attained a considerable fortune by playing cards.

PORTRAIT OF

A POET

The poet Sylvan Hardemuth, who died several years ago, was one of the strangest figures in literary history. For the case of a man who was celebrated as a poet because he was misunderstood must be viewed as peculiar if not unique.

Hardemuth's real name was Alphons Schwerdt. His extraordinarily lucid perception in literary matters was revealed while he was still young. He used this judgment in astute critical essays, campaigning against certain selected poets of the turn of the century, whom he soon managed to silence. He thereupon also lapsed into silence, having deprived himself of his victims. Since no other victims seemed to offer themselves for the moment (he had no objections to, or rather no interest in, the general trend of contemporary literature), he made up his mind to write his own poetry, showing the same defects the critical condemnation of which had shed the best light on the art of his venomous pen.

Taking the nom de plume of Sylvan Hardemuth, he wrote a collection of verse. Upon its publication, the leading literary journal ran a demolishing critique which was so brilliant that readers greedily devoured Hardemuth's poetry in order to fully relish Schwerdt's assessment—if one cares to call it that.

One year later, a second volume of poems by Hardemuth appeared, and it was followed by Schwerdt's review, which must be described as simply epoch-making in the field of critical literature. This procedure was repeated again the following year, and it bade fair to become a literary institution; but this time, it failed, because the public, whose favor can never be relied on, liked the poems. The review, although wittier than ever, met with cool rejection; readers determined that, for all its masterful dialectics, the analysis was unfair and petty. Schwerdt was not prepared for such a reaction, and in his next volume of poems he chose a style that can only be called crassly derivative even by the then prevailing standards. The public, however, was enthusiastic, and voices of indignation were raised against the critique that soon followed the book.

The embittered Schwerdt then let Hardemuth indite a collection of neo-Baroque sonnets; to no avail: Hardemuth had become a minion of the public (which proved steady in its favor), and he enjoyed the utterly undesired aura of the great poet. His prestige was heightened by his refusal to make any personal appearances. In 1909, as some readers may recall, he was awarded the Nobel Prize.

This was too much for Schwerdt. Discouraged and misunderstood, he decided to carry the pseudoexistence of the invented poet ad absurdum. As Sylvan Hardemuth, he purchased a farm with arable land, stables, cattle, and all the paraphernalia. He settled here, penning one volume of verse after another, going backward through the stylistic development of the centuries. He had just composed a Homeric epic when his quill was plucked from his hand by death, which seemed to have waited devotedly until he had reached the origins.

In between these works, Hardemuth occasionally wrote small articles for weekly journals, praising the silent simplicity of country life, the callowness of the rustic population, the beauty of the mountains in various seasons, and the down-to-earth dignity of the cattle. Driven by injured vanity, even brilliant people sometimes go too far. For it must unfortunately be said that these articles, while obviously written in moments of diabolical satisfaction, were taken quite seriously by the public; indeed, for a time, it almost looked as if the educated strata were about to return to nature. But things did not reach this pass; not even the influence of a Hardemuth was powerful enough.

Hardemuth tried once more to be Alphons Schwerdt, this time in a rather distasteful article, which claimed that the whole farming flimflam had no other function than to convince visitors of a mellow introspectiveness that is actually nothing but a pack of lies: the farmer, said Hardemuth, only pretended to farm, the farmhands were played by unemployed actors, and the herds were filled with mock-up cows made of painted plywood. This—to be sure, truly ridiculous —attack only aroused more mirth. It was seen—to some extent, correctly—as the infuriated, impotent raging of a dwarf against a giant. Schwerdt then fell silent as Schwerdt forever.

But now, Hardemuth—for we may henceforth call him that —settled more and more into his titanic role as he grew older, forgetting, or at least repressing, his earlier identity. Not only did the freedom he had gradually acquired enable him to leap about from one era to another in his poetry (truly a rhapsode of eclecticism!), but he now adjusted his daily life more and more to his poetic existence. He received his countless visitors, sitting in a high armchair, with a toga around his shoulders and a plaid blanket over his knees, a pose he copied from the traditional depictions of the princes of poets, who, as we know, must protect themselves against drafts in order to ensure their immortality. He also surrounded himself with disciples, male and female, who sat at his feet, on cushions (he called them "disciple cushions"), and addressed him as "master." A portrait painted just a few years before his death shows him in his armchair, with a quill in his left hand, a roll of parchment in his right hand; a bitterly delicate smile flits across his face as though he were forgiving the spectator in advance for any misjudgments he might eventually utter about him, Hardemuth. This painting is in my possession. I purchased it from a national gallery for a decent price, at a time when Hardemuth—not long after his death—turned out to be identical with Schwerdt, whereupon he fell into posthumous and definitive disgrace with the public, which felt painfully deceived.

In a few years, Hardemuth will be consigned to oblivion, a fate that very few Nobel laureates have been spared. When Hardemuth is forgotten, Schwerdt will be also forgotten, for the two cancel one another out.

THE TWO SOULS

The daily gazettes recently reported on a lawsuit that kept not only legal circles in suspense but also people interested in literature. The writer Hubertus Golch had brought libel charges against the critic Eduard Wiener, who made extremely pejorative remarks about him and his tragedy *Orestes* on the occasion of its premiere. Wiener, we were told, had nonobjective motives when he wrote that nowadays Agamemnon's family had to put up with anything a playwright had to say and, in this case, with what he should have had enough tact and self-criticism not to say. Golch, according to Wiener, was the last link in a chain of lamentable epigoni; in short, the accusations were the kind that no serious writer cares to endure. The trial began, and during this early phase, it turned out, much to the surprise of all parties, that Golch and Wiener were one and the same. In an attack of self-critical contrition, Golch had chosen this radical method to challenge publicly the value of his entire output.

The astonished court then recessed in order to consider what to do: this lovingly prepared lawsuit, which both the attorneys and the public had looked forward to, could not simply be dropped without further ado. Some precedence was sought. An elderly expert in libel cases recalled a—actually the single—case of this nature; a suit that had spelled a great deal of trouble for the courts in the previous century: the case of *Ansorge* v. *Ansorge* before the Grand Ducal Supreme Court of Karlsruhe. The reader will scarcely remember that curious affair unless he is in his eighties today. I, however, can still recall the matter, for I am over ninety; furthermore, the litigant was my cousin.

The philosopher Crispin Ansorge had, to put it in common parlance, two souls in his breast: he was a philosopher and a person. As a philosopher, he dealt, as befitted him, exclusively with the world of thought, never taking into account the world of emotions. As a person, however, he was averse to any sort of philosophy, since, as he said, it was, in its ultimate and strictest form, alien to feelings and thus to life. The fact that as a philosopher he represented dualistic tendencies, i.e., that the one-half of his split personality had a further split, may have exacerbated his internal dichotomy; but, in connection with this account, that is neither here nor there. In his favor, it must be said that during his lectures he never tried to attack other philosophical schools in order to force his listeners to accept his school as the only valid one. His lectures were like his thinking: measured and never torn by passion. The latter surfaced in the conflict between philosophy and life. Here, he fought an uncompromising struggle. Anyone meeting him on the street could never tell which of the two souls in his breast was to be addressed; indeed, things came to such a pass that if anyone wishing to visit him asked whether Herr Professor Ansorge was in, his housekeeper would reply, "Do you mean the thinker or the person?" Naturally, the ingenuous visitor was unprepared for such a dilemma; he would get confused and perhaps forgo the conversation altogether. In an unimportant person, such behavior would have been called nonsensical.

As a close relative of this peculiar person, I would like to dwell briefly on his family background. His father's character combined a certain unbridled imagination with unsophisticated naïveté. For a time, he fought for the reintroduction of jus primae noctis, which, quite unambivalently, indicates what a strange private world this man lived in, and also points to the fact that his son took over little if any of this paternal propensity, which, after all, presumes a certain, albeit chiefly theoretical, preoccupation with the body. The mother, in contrast, was happy by nature, down to earth, with both feet planted firmly on that earth. However, she was supposedly hard to take, for she seldom came out with anything but standard idioms and sayings, so that in her later years she never said anything that she had not always said. They may not have been your everyday couple; still, it would be pointless to seek a basis for the son's makeup in their personalities, no matter how quixotic their mixture of features, unless the parents had much deeper traits that, sublimating in him, then saw the light of day.

I have already mentioned the nature of his conflicts. The

fact that he did not teach what he lived (or vice versa) is something he shares with many philosophers. However, his situation was more extreme: as a person actively involved in the intellectual currents of the day, he commented on his own philosophy by fighting it with all means at his disposal, especially the press (though not the academic journals, which were not open to him as a person). In the heated, exaggerated diction he used (as a person), he advocated what he called the human standpoint vis-à-vis philosophy, which standpoint, however, he as a philosopher had to reject as unobjective. One may shrug off these articles, one may be offended by their agitated rhetoric, but one cannot doubt that they expressed the opinion of an upright man, who was very serious about what he was doing. The audience open to such problems was torn into a maelstrom of contrary opinions; and some people would have gladly taken part in this debate had they known how to go about defending Ansorge without attacking him at the same time. For one could never tell in which guise he might appear. No one wanted to expose himself to the philosopher's nasty sarcasm by taking up the cudgels for the person. So people held their tongues and let him fight it out with himself.

However, the polemics eventually became so extreme, their words so insulting, that one day Ansorge the person, who, unlike Ansorge the philosopher, frequently and also consciously acted in the heat of passion, brought a lawsuit against the latter. One can understand this only as his intention to have his action viewed as symbolic. In any case, it was a unique state of affairs.

The legal authorities, in this case, deserve our utmost respect. One cannot deny their benevolent cooperation in ticklish situations. Ansorge managed to arouse the enthusiasm of the counsel for each side, and thus came the trial that a major contemporary jurisprudent described as "the four-leaf clover on the meadow of libel litigation." In those days, people still used lovely images, usually plucking them from nature.

With cool composure, Ansorge repeatedly exchanged the plaintiff's seat for the defendant's. It already looked as if the person would win the case, for the mood on the judge's bench was leaning in his favor, and who would make a court liable for partisanship with humanity?! But now, the plaintiff was cross-examined by the defendant. Since Ansorge could not, after all, occupy both seats at once, the defendant's chair remained empty. Crispin Ansorge, who, in any event, could be certain of the triumph of one part of his personality, made a grand gesture toward the plaintiff's seat, turned to the judge and the public, and cried with dramatic dignity: "The person, that cowardly craven, has taken flight from the philosopher!" That was the high point. The applause was tempestuous, the wave of favor tumbled, at least for an instant, from humanity to philosophy. Socrates would have smirked. I too would like to have been there. Be that as it may, the person lost the case and was ordered to pay nominal damages. I do not know whether my cousin played out the comedy to the point of writing himself a check. In any event, the affair had an aftermath, in that the two attorneys, who had gotten more and more provoked at one another, brought suits against each other, which, so far as I know, were never settled.

Ansorge died by his own hand several years later. He no doubt wanted to make it look as if he had fallen victim to a duel with himself, whereby it is not clear which of the two—the person or the thinker—was to be considered the instigator. Both were dead, for his philosophical writings did not survive the person any more than his dualism has survived modern-day pluralism.

Since, we all know, Golch the writer also won his lawsuit against the critic with the alias of Wiener, we can draw the lesson that in such cases (which I would like to call double-soul cases in order to coin a precedence term for any future eventualities), the defendant's soul carries the day over the plaintiff's soul.

The reader, whose sense of justice is satisfied by such a circumstance, should, however, be told that this thesis, as we have emphasized, must be viewed as empirical. It is based not on moral, but purely on jurisprudential necessity, and it therefore, regrettably, loses its ethical substance.

WESTCOTTE'S RISE

AND FALL

Rudolf Westcotte was inspired. He realized this very early and accepted it with placid calm; while still young, he already knew he would be spared the fate of those who view the deep, dark drive for self-expression as a sublime vocation. He therefore countered the generosity of the Muses without the humility for which the titans of art are credited (for the most part, mistakenly); rather, he felt he deserved it all, and he made a point of beating the top representatives of the fine arts, each at his own game. At the age of twenty-two, he placed the final and decisive accents on easel painting in his time, after which he picked up the chisel, using a few well-aimed strokes to correct the—by his lights, imperfect— state of sculpture. He then casually turned to the fresco, creating immortal works on the walls of major public buildings, only to turn casually away again. (He had taken care of the graphic arts during his creative recesses.)

Thus, his fellow artists were competitively conquered, and the traditional means of expression exhausted. Having sullenly decided to give up art or, as the Germans put it, hang it up on a nail, Westcotte, a lover of symbols, drove a nail into the wall of his studio. This, however, was one of those turning points of which—if we are to put faith in biographers—there is at least one in the life of every real artist; you see, the hammering woke up Bettina, who was sleeping in the next room. Bewildered, she hurried over; familiar with her husband's delight in symbols, she instantly divined the meaning of the nail.

Bettina was ambitious, and thus unwilling to forgo the polychrome glory that reflected her in fashion magazines as a famous beauty and in critical works as her famous husband's noblest model: a coupling of two functions, which gave substance to her life. She had thus always assured herself of a seamless chronicle of her ripening beauty by getting Rudolf to capture her forms and features with pencil, brush, or chisel, depending on the stage he happened to be in. It is therefore understandable that she vehemently protested against his resolution to lay down his tools.

"My dear, if the tried-and-true media," she called to him, "do not suffice for you, then take this." She pressed a pair of pruning shears into his hand. "Go out into the garden and clip my portrait into the boxwood hedge!"

Wordlessly, Rudolf took the shears, went outside, and began to create an over-life-sized portrait of his wife in the boxwood. Bettina's idea had rekindled the seemingly guttering fire. Brilliant people often need the slightest hint in regard to an untried area, and they are already aroused from their lethargy.

Topiary is an art form that imposes a certain architectural simplification on its creator. But then, stylized reduction to essentials had always been Rudolf Westcotte's forte and philosophy. The portrait turned out well. It was followed by likenesses of selected friends. He left the theoretical underpinnings to the pack of his biographers, to whom the discovery of this unhoped-for virgin soil offered a welcome opportunity for self-aggrandizing elaboration.

However, this period did not last for long either. Since boxwood hedges grow quickly, they require constant revision of their profiles. Rudolf did not care to prune his existing works day after day. He therefore resolved to let the now stately gallery keep growing, much to the annoyance of Bettina, whose portrait, in an advanced state of neglect, had degenerated into a snide caricature. In her agitation, she tried to save her effigy, but failed. Under her violent trimming, the bush shrank to a skeleton. The couple left on a trip in order to escape its final stages of unruliness. This also spelled the end of that period.

Arriving in Marseilles, they thought of sailing to Samoa. But something very different happened. One night, as they were walking along the Canebière, Rudolf bumped into a new turning point: a drunken, half-naked sailor. The couple managed to elude his dangerous purview in the nick of time. But as the man reeled by, they saw his torso in the light of a streetlamp: it was densely covered with pictures, like a wall in the Louvre. "You should learn how to tattoo people!" said Bettina, excited by this spectacle. "I think you could do great things, Rudolf!"

Rudolf's inner voice repeated Bettina's idea. Within a week, he had learned the craft in the harbor of Marseilles. In exchange for a generous tuition fee, a master put several sailors at his disposal, men who were not so sensitive as to become angry about an occasional revision. Soon, Rudolf became practiced with the needle, which he now applied to Bettina's precious back.

Once again, the muses did not fail. The picture on Bettina's back was a masterpiece of buoyant transparency, a composition in bright, airy tones. For Westcotte, whose imagination had been promptly kindled by the new, flexible material, managed to transcend the primitive linearity that had always been inherent in the art of tattooing; he, the master of the great vision, succeeded in adding colored surfaces by breaking through the traditional frame and involving the shoulder blades up to the armpits in the composition. This procedure did cause Bettina a few hours of friction, slightly palliated by strong drugs; but the result was smart money enough. When, having fully recovered, she used several mirrors to view the effectiveness of the new adornment, her joy was great.

Needless to say, the two of them never used their boat tickets; instead, they went to the Riviera. Here, people knew how important Westcotte was, and soon after the women on the beach had a glimpse of Bettina, Rudolf could turn to new backs.

Great art is the expression of a kind of supertruth; there

is something greater and more convincing about it than our prosaic reality, which eludes the possibility of artistic depiction because of its recurrent workaday banality. This super-truth characterizes Westcotte's backs, the most mature of which probably belongs to Mrs. Homer B. Shrankle, Jr.: a horizontal still life in dark-brown and dull-red nuances, emanating peace and quiet, masterful in the harmony of its tonal values. Supposedly, the Museum of Modern Art of New York is negotiating for this piece with the heirs of the not so young Mrs. Shrankle, as it did for the back of the old Marquise de Corvois-Dutour, whose heirs, according to some malicious scuttlebutt, do not exactly sleep on a bed of roses. But granted, we all know how rumor exaggerates in precisely such matters!

The first exhibit of Westcotte's back pictures took place in Cannes. It was a benefit show, and since ladies of high society are willing to do anything for charitable purposes, they made themselves available to the committee with a selflessness revealing a true social conscience: three hours a day, they sat in the gallery, wearing robes with plunging backlines, their backs toward the public which filed past. However, these ladies had stipulated that they would sit behind glass to avoid investigations of texture and pigment by experts intent on close analysis.

Westcotte wandered past the rows of his works—dissatisfied; he felt that the stiff and static quality of his compositions was not up to the material. One should, he thought to himself, adjust the technical possibilities to the living matter: the picture should be forever moving, in changing, iridescent harmony; forms and planes had to alter one another, a permanent ebb and flow of light and shadow, cheerful and exuberant. The thought of having his women do gymnastics did not appeal to him: it would have surpassed all reasonable boundaries. Besides, this would have been the wrong path to the ideal unity he desired. No, the living pictures that now emerged in his mind's eye required a new conception involving all possibilities of movement. He had to pursue this idea.

He whispered good-bye to Bettina, who was among the exhibited women, and he left town, hoping to devote himself to his new task in a new environment.

The season was over. The half-empty lobby of the huge hotel was filled with sunny drowsiness. Here and there, a mocha spoon clinked softly through the rustle of weary after-dinner conversation. All at once, a woman in a strapless summer frock emerged from a group of guests and made her way to the piano.

Her name was Hedwig Wiesendanck; she was a medium-talented concert pianist, but she also had solid artistic principles that did not permit her to expose her art to the dubious public of Swiss spas, much as she had always enjoyed being constantly urged by some of the members of that audience. Today, however, after properly hesitating, she gave in to their urging, for she knew that a powerful man was in the lobby, a great demolisher of all principles: Hernando Rosenbarth, the international impresario, who frequently, following a jovial whim, had raised a doughty performer from the anonymity of local charity events to the light of the headlines.

43

Hedwig Wiesendanck opened the piano. Conversation died out, the mocha spoon was left on the saucer. Hedwig first played a few of her own paraphrases, which served to offer timid—and unfortunately useless—proof that the interpreter also had her creative side. These pieces were strictly tonal, nay, downright classical, yet so imaginative that the guests always exchanged meaningful nods as if to say: "Why, fancy that! She's really something!"

Next, she played Chopin, whereby, true to the mimetic tradition, she emphasized the rubato by ardently shaking her head. A few guests tiptoed out of the lobby, followed by pitying or irked glances from other guests: lowbrows!

Ordinarily, Rudolf would have left the lobby; not because he didn't care for music; on the contrary, because he preferred listening to it when he felt like it and when he could select the performer himself. But today, he remained. The pianist had a beautiful back; the interplay of muscles and shoulder blades fascinated him. When she was done, he went over to her, accompanied by the glances of those who recognized him.

"Mademoiselle, you have a beautiful back," he said, for he could afford not to beat around the bush. Hedwig blushed deeply. The unusual compliment was unexpected. Furthermore, she did not know from whom it came. Concert artists are seldom informed about anything but the impact made by other concertizing musicians, their potential rivals. Meanwhile, before Hedwig Wiesendanck pulled herself together again, Westcotte made his offer, and before she could reply, Hernando Rosenbarth also made her an offer, from the other side, on condition, however, that she accept Westcotte's proposal.

For Rosenbarth had instantly recognized Westcotte, knowing who and what he was, and able to express his worth in figures. And he could instantly see Hedwig Wiesendanck in crowded concert halls, turning her mobile, parti-colored back to an enthusiastic audience.

The morning after Hedwig Wiesendanck's first concert, the art world agreed that Westcotte had reached his acme. Such a combination of visionary impact with the sovereign mellowness of almost a work of old age (as the reviews put it) could not be surpassed even by a Westcotte. The traditional statements about the significance and quality of the études, mazurkas, and sonatas were limited to an infinitesimal few; the interpretation was not even deigned worthy of mention.

A few days after the concert, Hedwig invited Rudolf to tea. They sat in her small, tasteful sitting room, among leafy plants, Franz Marc reproductions, and handwoven cushion covers.

"The tea is divine," said Rudolf.

"Darjeeling," said Hedwig.

"But there's something else in it, something that gives it its special aroma."

"That," said Hedwig, "is poison."

Rudolf leaned back pleasurably and drained his cup. Then he said: "I have done my task. Why, I recently asked myself over and over whether what I have done was really my task, or whether I went too far in giving the mortal coils of several people a material value that does not become them. But you, Fräulein Wiesendanck: You had a wonderful future ahead of you."

"I still *do,*" said Hedwig with the triumph of a wallflower that has grown into an unexpectedly marvelous blossom. "The poison is only in *your* cup. I, on the other hand, am beginning my first international tour tomorrow: as the *only* pianist with a Westcotte on her back."

Rudolf smiled. "And how much did he pay you to get rid of me?"

"Who?"

"Rosenbarth."

"Ten thousand."

"Too little," said Rudolf, putting down the cup and giving up the ghost.

Hedwig pulled out her blue-leather diary to preserve these last two words of the great artist for all eternity. The diary could, however, be opened only after her death. Then, she would be forgiven for the murder—for her back's sake, and she would enter eternity next to Westcotte. "Too little," she wrote.

But as she wrote, her deed and her motives dawned on her fully. In the face of these two words, her entire cruel lack of fulfillment emerged within her; her existence, not as an artist but as a handmaiden of the arts, not even great enough for a glorious ephemeralness; the hand of an immortal had only ennobled her mortal coils, and only one of the unnoble parts at that. "Too little!"

Gingerly, Hedwig Wiesendanck poured a few colorless

drops into her teacup. Then she carefully inserted the vial with the skull and crossbones into Rudolf's right hand. If they found it there, she thought, they might think that Rudolf Westcotte had wanted to join her, Hedwig Wiesendanck, in death. This was her final, desperate grab at a long-vanished dream of glory and fulfillment.

But this suspicion occurred to no one who so much as sensed Rudolf's importance or had ever heard Hedwig play the piano.

FROM MY DIARY

22 September. Event of the week: the exhibition of new picture frames by Mario Molé in the Kröller Gallery. Yesterday afternoon, opening, with sherry and excellent cheese sticks. The visitors again accepted the fact that the frames contained no paintings. They are, the catalog explains, so masterful as objects that any painting inside them would interfere with this sublime perfection, diverting the viewer's gaze.

The frame as an end in itself: the phrase *"l'art pour l'art"* perhaps in its most extreme form of application. A problem that almost seems to transcend pure aesthetics and that, no doubt, will be much discussed in the future by competent and, presumably, not so competent parties. The idea strikes me too as bold, while arousing contradiction, which, however, I did not express in the circle of guests; its formulation must first be mulled over. After all, I am no expert in these matters.

The pièce de résistance was no. 11: a horizontal stucco

frame in altrose, with a continuous acanthus decoration, concentrated in the corners, of gold foil, with a light patina. Molé supposedly worked on it for several years. It was bought by Consul Bellroth between two conversations, whereby he once again confirmed his surprisingly unerring sense of the exquisite. This little action was greeted by murmurs of acknowledgment. A few people even clapped, thus making him the symbolic manifestation of a certain moderate progressiveness, a demonstration of fine, genuine collectorhood.

Usteguy gave the address at the opening. He pointed out the significance of the picture frame for our cultural life. The picture frame (this was more or less his drift), if viewed in its figurative sense, is one of the connective existential entities of our existentially cognizant world, as, more or less, a positive equivalent of the latent but imminent fateful doom of an era that has lost the sense of transcendental values. Loud applause, in which the artist also joined. That, he said later, was precisely what he was trying to say with his frames (which I doubt, incidentally). Now if I remember correctly, Usteguy articulated similar thoughts in his essay "On Sports," mainly about fishing. How greatly the philosopher's equipment has increased in our time, not to mention the growing applicability of his theses! Nevertheless, one is enchanted by the seventy-nine-year-old's vitality, spellbound by his fascinating, yet absolutely compelling way of extending his empirical outlook to the picture frame. He has captured it, seen through it, like no one else. He was accompanied by two young ladies, in whom he seemed very interested.

I purchased a small frame, which I may fill with a still life.

.   .   .

25 September. Two invitations in the morning mail. One was from my bank, advising me to buy gilt-edged mortgage bonds paying five percent. Although I have never shown any sign of accepting such invitations, the bank, with stubborn friendliness, keeps asking me to take part in these or similar transactions, as if my reluctance has given me a favored-customer status. Yet I do not even know whether the mortgage they are referring to is my present one, my future one, or somebody else's altogether. In any case, I have no mortgage on my home, nor do I intend to take one out.

The other invitation is from the head of the German Bartschedel Society, asking me to give the memorial address at the unveiling of the monument for the bicentennial of Bartschedel's death, on October 14, in Osnabrück.

This is obviously a mistake. Nevertheless, I have decided to accept the invitation, since I have never attended the unveiling of a monument, much less given the commemorative address. I would therefore like to take advantage of this opportunity, since few monuments are unveiled nowadays. I have to find out as soon as possible who Bartschedel was.

Morning constitutional through the park: a bleak autumn day. The sky is gray, the leaves are yellow, a dead day, which the meager baby-carriage traffic is unable to animate.

I found a suitable painting for my newly purchased frame in an antique shop on Rosenow Strasse: a vegetable still life, freshly and ingenuously second-rate, probably Netherlandish, in any case imbued with the old Netherlandish love of prosaic details. Bulbs, stems, and leaves metallically clear, overly sharp in outline, as though cut out of colored silver foil, with the obligatory drop of dew; nor is the traditional insect missing: perched on a radish, it is neither a fly nor a bug, but The Insect per se. The surface of the painting is very dark, I have to clean it.

27 September. Morning in the National Library. I was somewhat astonished to find Gottfried Willibald Bartschedel described as a quack, an astrologer, and a generally fraudulent evangelist, who, as I gleaned from the reference work, pulled the wool over the eyes of his contemporaries, they being a bit overtaxed by the spirit of Enlightenment and therefore all the more receptive to the opposite pole. Of course, it instantly struck me that these data might no longer be consistent with the most recent state of Bartschedel scholarship; after all, the letterhead of the society sported a few names that have a rich, nay, ringing resonance in our academic world, and their bearers would vigorously resist cultivating the memory of a dubious figure. On the other hand, of course, it cannot be ruled out that the aim and goal of this society is the complete vindication of a controversial personality. After all, nowadays, people, especially academics, do a lot of vindicating or, if someone's honor can no longer be vindicated, they rehabilitate him. Bartschedel preached salvation, all well and good —but perhaps the salvation he preached was no worse than that promised by other men to whom monuments have been raised? In any case, I intend to keep my address as general as possible, for, as so often in life, I must be prepared for all eventualities.

This afternoon, I began to clean my vegetable still life with a mixture of benzine and turpentine. After several hours of cautious rubbing, the pigment began to vanish rather than gradually lightening up, as I had expected, and the oil sketch of a female head appeared underneath, no doubt from the Rubens School. Now I am no fan of Rubens, much less his school, which took over the worldly fleshliness of its idol—not without piety, to be sure, but far less convincingly. Besides, the Molé frame is not right for a female head.

I made up my mind to go to Casarina tomorrow in order to obtain an expert appraisal from Friedensohn, without which no old master—not even an old disciple—is to be sold today. Perhaps a visit to Tessino will also be beneficial to my Bartschedel address. I am certainly not getting anywhere here at home.

29 September, Casarina. The air here is still delightfully mild, and so I am taking up again the traces of summer, which always seems to slip through our fingers in these regions. Only the vintage festival, whose program is annually distributed throughout the weeks of the autumn season, with the possibilities of the grape as an object, foodstuff, and symbol being savored to the dregs, recalls that the year is waning in Tessino too; but it wanes with a graceful joie de vivre. Under the arcades of this picturesquely designed lakeside town, thoroughly workmanlike in its colorfulness and sedulousness, the late-season traveler to Italy stops his car, leans over toward his passengers, and says: "Actually, this is Italian enough, don't you think?" And the passengers agree, for here

they find themselves still within the borders of a multiply proven paradise and also on the right side of the hygiene frontier.

It is night. A warm wind wafts from the opposite shore, sheet lightning flashes over the San Benedetto, the lake and the trees murmur softly in the wind: this is just the right mood for tackling a commemoration speech. It is turning out in such a way that I can keep it for other occasions in case I show some promise in this field. I have decided to pick up on Usteguy's highly lucid idea and use it in my Bartschedel interpretation. In the fateful doom of our modern era, which has lost the sense of transcendental values, Bartschedel's legacy must appear chiefly as the connective existential entity of an existentially more cognizant cultural epoch. Therein lies his great merit—but also a certain risk of misinterpretation by the unqualified. So much for his work. And then the analysis of his personality, whereby, needless to say, I would like not only to go into his tragic dichotomy, but also to touch upon his quest for the mystical, without which an appreciation of this kind can scarcely be considered complete. The address is turning out well.

This morning, I rang up Friedensohn. I spoke with his secretary, who said *il conte* (I believe Friedensohn is a papal count) could not be disturbed. At my urgent pleading, she did agree to convey my request to him. In the afternoon, she called me back and asked me to send the painting over. Furthermore, *il conte* would expect me for tea that same afternoon.

.   .   .

30 September, Casarina. My painting is not by a Rubens disciple, it is an early Rubens, indeed a preliminary study for his *Allegory of War* from the year 1637. This was revealed to me by Friedensohn as he received me in his study. I thereupon asked him whether he might care to buy it. He waved me off, saying, "Dear friend, you must know that old Friedensohn" (smiling modestly, he replaced the nobility title with an allusion to his age and thus virtually to his infamous cunning as a connoisseur) "that old Friedensohn buys only the Tuscan School—and only the best at that, only the best!

"Incidentally," he added, standing up, "I have always found the Netherlands too prosaic in their subject matter, too homespun." He made a face as if he had tasted a morsel that he would never have tolerated at his renowned epicurean table.

We then stepped into the garden, where tea was served under acacias and chestnut trees that were still a full, splendid green. Here, the secretary discreetly handed me a sealed envelope on the back of which the Friedensohn coat of arms shone resplendent. (I have just opened it. It contains the invoice for his appraisal.)

One of the guests was Usteguy, accompanied by two young ladies; not the same ones who had accompanied him to the opening, but he was no less attentive to these two. He was coming from an international track-and-field competition in Bologna, where he had given the welcoming address. He was cheerful, well tanned, and did not restrain his guttural utterances of well-being. These philosophers certainly know how to live. In this area alone, one can learn a great deal from them.

4 October. Home since the day before yesterday. Immediately after my return, I set about cleansing the final remains of the vegetable still life from my Rubens, but before the former vanished at the edges, the female head began to dissolve in the middle, to reveal an Upper Bavarian mountain landscape in the twilight of the waning day. It shows, if my memory for landscapes does not deceive me, the area around Oberammergau. I cannot deny that I was a wee bit irked by this unexpected multiplicity of strata. For, naturally, such a subject is even less proper for Molé's frame than a female head.

I instantly wrote to Friedensohn, informing him of his error and explaining to him that, under the circumstances, I was not willing to pay the rather considerable price for his appraisal.

I would, incidentally, like to know what might be hidden behind the *Judgment of Paris* that the National Gallery purchased some time ago at Friedenson's behest. The dimensions of this painting inspire conjectures of enormous panoramas, whose artistic quality, however, if equivalent to that of my painting, would transfer the *Judgment* from the area of art to that of local artifact. Of course, such doubts may be exaggerated: an unfortunate discovery like mine leads to a pessimistic outlook in matters of art history.

Yesterday evening, a concert. Wörthwanger conducting his second symphony. I admire his fidelity and scrupulous devotion to the Romantics from Schubert to Bruckner in immaculate stylistic purity. Except for the last movement, when Puccini made a rather sudden appearance, which I found to be quite a break in the style, albeit the only one, for the applause was thunderous: as though each person had recognized his favorite composer and was ardently thanking the performer for a profound, but deliciously simple imitation.

16 October. Returned from Osnabrück yesterday. My address at the unveiling of the monument was a great success, and my veneration as the greatest living Bartschedel scholar was almost embarrassing. I managed to conceal my anxiety and tension during the speech, for needless to say, I expected at any moment to find myself face-to-face with the man who deserved, and had expected to be asked, to give the memorial speech on the basis of his actual scholarship. However, he was absent, and the enigma is as yet unsolved. I suspect that the man is my namesake, and also hardworking, tireless, and inexperienced in the ways of the world, a man who, after a life of the most abstemious withdrawal and quiet scholarly labor, recognized by only a select handful, passed away inconspicuously, mourned, if at all, then by an old housekeeper, who did not know whom to turn to with the news of his decease and the countless pages of his almost completed life's work.

Incidentally, the celebrant, as I then found out, was not Gottfried Willibald Bartschedel, but Christian Theodor Bartschedel, whom I had not reached while leafing through the reference work, since I did not suspect that there was a second bearer of this last name. I cannot deny that I was overcome by a feeling of having acted irresponsibly. But a glance in the encyclopedia this morning put me at ease. Christian Theodor Bartschedel's merits are entirely more general than those of Gottfried Willibald Bartschedel, whose achievements are, and—presumably—will remain, highly controversial, as is only fitting for a quack, an astrologer, and a fraudulent evangelist.

Christian Theodor Bartschedel, in contrast, was an important educator and philanthropist, a courageous champion of so-called general education (a term he coined), a pioneer in the field of evening courses, a Pestalozzi for adults. It strikes me as a sign of the times that life no longer brings one into contact with such names.

17 October. Last night, a storm stripped all the leaves off the trees, turning the green outside my windows into a latticework of naked branches. The decisive changes of the year occur suddenly, usually overnight. And thus, the weeks have finally come when the poetry columns of our newspapers are filled with glum insights and gloomy inklings to which people blindly and blithely shut off their senses in cheerier seasons.

Two letters in the mail. One from my bank, containing a proposal for a profitable transaction; the other from Friedensohn. He writes:

> Dearest friend,
>   You have written to me that after working on your painting, you discovered, beneath the Rubens sketch, a mountain landscape that, in your opinion, was painted

in the twentieth century and, as you then go on, is not one of the best works that this century has produced. You have asked me, in view of this state of affairs, to refrain from charging you for my appraisal. Well, I am willing to comply with your request, but I cannot hold back a certain rebuke.

You have robbed yourself of an item of value by giving in to a—I might say, childish—scholarly urge: the urge to know what is behind something. This was not wise of you. Furthermore, it is unwonted. Where would we be today, I ask you, if we left a place for petty doubts in our scholarship, whose goal, after all, is to determine the major directions and put them in order!

We art experts are supposed to preserve concepts of value and create new ones whenever the old are lost. My assessment gave you an article of value which it was in your interest to preserve. Instead, you did research on your own by washing away the layer of pigments. And now you complain to me that underneath, a mountain landscape has emerged rather than the naked canvas. Please do not take offense, dear friend, but that is really not my fault.

Yours very truly,
Francesco Friedensohn

With sophisticated modesty, he once again omitted his title. Incidentally, I do not quite understand the tenor of his letter; I did not complain to him in any way. I would never even dream of complaining to old Friedensohn, who, after all, like Usteguy or Wörthwanger, is one of the grand old men of our culture.

THE INSURANCE

AGENT'S GUEST

PERFORMANCE

Anyone who has ever heard the pianist František Hrdla play will never forget his enormous impact (no
matter how hard one may try). His breathtaking vivacity and
virtuoso technique have inspired the greatest critics of our
century to compare him to Anton Rubinstein; and Eduard
Watznik, the nestor of the music writers (he is 104 years old
today, but, although occasionally confusing opus numbers,
still at the height of his receptive powers)—Watznik once
exclaimed: "If you close your eyes, you think you are listening to Liszt!" In London and Cairo, Paris and Williamsburgh,
Pa.—everywhere, this divinely gifted musician is overwhelmed with frantic applause at the fading of his final note.
Then, thoroughly drained, he rises slowly, though modestly:
merely a servant to the work of the composer. He takes a deep
bow, whereby, it is said, a weary smile flickers at the corners
of his mouth. A genuine artist, the ingenuous concertgoer
thinks, a true darling of the Muses! Only very few people,

including myself, his boyhood friend, know about his tragedy, the cause of his weary smile: Hrdla is a frustrated insurance agent.

František Maria Hrdla comes from a family of musicians. His father was greatly in demand as a music teacher, whose four-handed versions of the classics are of inestimable value to home music. (As a composer, to be sure, he was nothing more than "capable," and his symphonies are forgotten today.) His mother was one of six daughters of Johann Nepomuk Hummel, but as a harpist she conquered her own position in musical life.

No sooner had little František outgrown the cradle than he was placed on the piano stool; by the age of four, he had *The Cheerful Countryman* behind him, and four years later, he could be measured for the velvet pants of the child prodigy. This anxious development was suddenly halted: by chance, young František got to know an insurance agent, who managed to arouse a deep interest in insurance within the ten-year-old.

Thus began the conflict the full scope of which can be understood only by the reader whose own youthful destiny was to struggle for a remote ideal against an uncomprehending and inexorable father. It is not without deep sympathy that one pictures the nerve-racking guilt feelings of the young man, who was forced to meet agents and statisticians in secret, since his all-too-strict father forbade him to have any dealings with representatives of such professions. Nevertheless, as František later confessed to me, the period in which he read Baumgartner's *Legal Practice in Insurance Matters* under his covers at night and wrote his own—incidentally, quite appealing—essay, "Cash Flow and Overhead," was one of the happiest in his life.

But no truly sensitive person can long endure such a lasting strain on his resistance. Defeated and discouraged, young František was forced to submit to his fate; he soon began a triumphal procession through the world, never garnering anything but laurels. I lost touch with him for years, but whenever I saw his picture in the newspapers, it seemed to me as if his weary gaze had a touch of painful renunciation, a profound yearning for a long-vanished ideal.

Yesterday, for the first time in many years, I heard him perform after his return from a foreign tour: he played Malinczewsky's Ninth Piano Concerto, which, just like the preceding eight concerti, is dedicated to Hrdla. He played so divinely that total strangers shook hands with one another and even a hard-boiled expert like myself had a tear in his eye.

During the recess, before the Eroica, I plied my way with my umbrella through the excited swarm of autograph hunters into the artist's dressing room. My friend František, aged, tired, and spent, sat among laurel wreaths, picking them apart with an absent gaze. Striding over to him, I kissed him on both cheeks and said that his playing had been a revelation. He coolly asked whether I had expected anything else. That, I cried out excitedly, is the only way to play Malinczewsky. It was nonsense, I went on, to claim that this composer requires no rubato or change of tempo. The restrained touch, the exaggerated motoricity of the so-called Objective School of pianists. . . . But he was not listening, he kept looking askance at me. I paused. Was this the lurking look of the insurance agent, glancing at a new risk? A bit confused, I kept talking, now about his rare combination of brillant technique and true expressiveness. My words left him cold.

I felt as if I were wasting my breath; disillusioned, I got to my feet, shook his hand, and was about to leave in order to clear the way for the storm of autograph collectors. František suddenly asked with cautious composure: "Listen, old friend, are you insured?"

Somewhat huskily, I admitted I wasn't.

His eyes lit up; he was awake and excited. Leaping over to the table, he took several policies from the drawer. Before I could say "Eroica," he had insured me against murder, accidents, hail and fog, and all misdeeds, catastrophes, and acts of God that one can be insured against. I shall never forget those minutes; his wonderful oratory and his warm rhetoric truly vied with the primal force of his piano playing.

Clutching the signed policy, I took my leave. He called after me, "Send in the autograph collectors!" and pulled a thick pile of papers from the drawer. I do not like saying it, but the last look he gave me was like a grin.

A strange person, I thought during the Eroica, truly, a double talent of unwonted proportions.

WHY I CHANGED INTO A NIGHTINGALE

I have changed into a nightingale out of conviction. Since neither the motives nor the decision relating to this deed are of a routine nature, I feel that the history of my metamorphosis is worth recounting.

My father was a zoologist, who spent his life inditing a multivolumed opus (lauded in professional circles) on amphibians, since he considered the literature in this field inadequate and to some extent defective. It may have been wrong of me, but I was never really interested in his work, even though our home had a lot of frogs and salamanders, whose habits and development would have justified a study.

My mother had been an actress before her marriage, reaching her acme, but never surpassing it, in a portrayal of Ophelia at the Public Theater of Zwickau. It is owing to this fact that I was christened Laertes, a euphonious but somewhat farfetched name. Still and all, I was grateful to her for not naming me Polonius or Guildenstern, though now it no longer makes any difference, of course.

When I was five years old, my parents gave me a magician's set. I learned how to do conjuring tricks of sorts—albeit on a child's limited scale—before I could even read or write. With the powders and instruments in this set, one could turn colorless water red and then colorless again, or one could take a wooden egg and turn it over, whereby it split in two, one half vanishing without a trace; one could pull a piece of cloth through a ring, whereby the cloth changed color. In short, (and this is true of most toys), there was nothing in the game that represented a miniature of reality; indeed, the manufacturer of this fantasy tool seemed intent on utterly ignoring the educational goal and suppressing a child's budding interest in practical applications. This fact had a decisive influence on my later development, for the pleasure of turning one useless object into another useless object taught me that I should seek happiness in knowledge without desire. Still, I never found this happiness prior to my transformation.

Now, however, my ambition was jogged. Soon, my magic set no longer sufficed, for I had meanwhile learned how to read and, on the cover of my set, I read the degrading words "The Little Conjurer."

I can still recall the afternoon when I went into my father's study to ask him if I could take magic lessons. Absorbed in the world of amphibians, he looked at me absentmindedly. I made my request; he instantly agreed. I cannot help thinking that he assumed I meant piano lessons, which can be gleaned from the fact that he would ask me for some time whether I was already playing Czerny études. I said I was, for I was certain I would not have to demonstrate what I told him.

I thus took magic lessons from a magician who performed on various vaudeville stages in our town and also, as he told me, had successfully appeared in London and Paris. Within a few years (I was already attending high school), I had learned enough to spirit rabbits out of a high hat. With great pleasure, I can remember my first performance, which I gave to an audience of parents and relatives. My parents were proud of my ability, which I had acquired peripherally, so to speak, and which I would henceforth pursue as a hobby in lieu of music next to my future profession (of which they had no specific idea). But I had other plans.

I had outgrown my magic teacher and was now experimenting on my own. But I was not withal neglecting my general education. I read a great deal and associated with my schoolmates, observing their development. One, for example, who had been given an electric train in his childhood, was preparing for a career as a railroad official; another, who had played with tin soldiers, opted for the life of an army officer. Thus did early influence regulate the job market, and each person chose his profession—or rather, the profession chose him. I, however, resolved to arrange my life according to entirely different considerations.

I would like to point out that in the decisions I made during the next few years, I was not led by the idea of being thought of as an eccentric or even an original. It was rather the growing realization that one cannot simply choose a career in the bourgeois sense without somehow trespassing on someone else's preserve. That was why a career as a public official struck me as particularly immoral. But I also rejected other professions, which are considered more humanitarian. I even found the work of a physician to be dubious, for, while he can save a man's life, the saved man might be an out-and-out villain, whose death was fervently desired by hundreds of downtrodden wretches.

Along with this insight, I also realized that some facts can be gleaned only from the momentary state of things, and it is useless to draw any conclusions or derive any experience from them. I therefore resolved to spend my life inactively and to think about nothing. I acquired two toads, lay down on a chaise longue, and observed the birds overhead and the toads underfoot. I had given up magic, for I had reached perfection. I felt capable of turning people into animals. I made no use of this ability, for I believed I could not justify such interference in someone else's life.

It was during this period that I first felt the wish to become a bird. Initially, I did not really care to admit this wish to myself, for it signified something like a defeat. I thus had not yet managed to take utter joy in the existence of birds; my feeling was dimmed by my yearning. Nevertheless, I was weak enough to toy with the idea of carrying out my wish, nay, I was even proud of being able to make it come true if and when I wanted; all it would take was a test of my skill.

This opportunity soon knocked. One afternoon, when I was lying in the garden, observing my toads, I received a visit from my friend, Dr. Werhahn. He was a newspaper editor. (As a boy, he had been given a printing press.) He lay down on the chaise longue next to mine and began to complain, first about the nastiness of newspaper readers, then about the inadequacy of present-day journalism. I said nothing, for people do not like being interrupted while complaining. Finally he concluded, "I'm fed up." And as one of my toads crept out from beneath his chaise longue, he added, "I wish I were a toad." Those were his last words, for I took my magic wand and transformed him. Thus ended Dr. Werhahn's journalistic career, though his life was probably lengthened by his transformation, since toads live to a ripe old age. But for me, it was a success. Furthermore, I now had three toads. (To forestall any suspicion, I would like to assure my readers that I had bought the other two as animals.)

Prior to my own metamorphosis, I applied my skill one more time. I recall this occasion not without a certain disquiet, for I am not quite sure whether I acted properly.

One afternoon in June, after spending the day in the country, I was sitting under a linden tree in the garden of a tavern, drinking a glass of apple cider. I enjoyed my solitude. But soon a flock of five young girls came into the garden and sat down at the next table. These girls looked fresh and nice, but I was displeased at the disturbance and became more displeased when they began to sing, with one of them accompanying the song on a mandolin. First they sang, "I must go, I must go from the town, from the town . . . ," and then:

> If I were a bird,
> And if I had two wings,
> I would fly to thee.

I have always found this song rather silly, especially since the two wings are a bird's natural appurtenance anyway. But now it was the articulated wish to be a bird that inspired me to terminate the singing and transform the songstresses into a flock of swallows. I went over to their table and waved my magic wand, possibly conveying the momentary impression that I wanted to conduct this quintet—but not for long. Five sparrows rose aloft and flew away amidst shrieks. Only five half-empty beer glasses, several chewed-on slices of bread and butter, and the fallen mandolin (a still life that left me slightly dismayed) testified that young lives had been in full flower here just a few seconds earlier.

Faced with this devastation, I was overcome by a slight sense of regret, for I thought to myself that the desire to be a bird may not have been immediately and unequivocally expressed by the singing of the song, and that furthermore the phrase, "If I were a bird," did not necessarily signify the wish to be one, although this is, of course, the drift of the song (so far as one may speak of a drift in such a song). I felt that I had acted in the heat of passion, under the influence of my (certainly quite justified) aversion. I considered this unworthy of myself, and I therefore made up my mind not to put off my own transformation any longer. I would like to emphasize that it was not the fear of consequences for my deed, perhaps criminal prosecution, that impelled me to finally assume a different shape. (After all, had I been arrested, how easily I could have turned the police detectives into pet terriers or the like!) It was actually the certitude that, for technical reasons, I would never achieve the peace and quiet I needed in order to enjoy things purely and undimmed by my will. Somewhere or other, a dog would always bark, a baby cry, or a young girl sing. The body of a nightingale was not an arbitrary choice. I wanted to be a bird because the thought of flying from treetop to treetop was very alluring. I also wanted to sing, for I loved music. Naturally, I weighed the possibility of becoming the one who interferes with someone else's life by disturbing his sleep. But now that I am no longer a human being, the thoughts and interests of human beings would never occur to me. My ethics are the ethics of a nightingale.

Last September, I stepped into my bedroom, opened the window wide, transformed myself, and flew away. I have never regretted it.

Now it is May. Twilight is setting in, evening is coming. Soon it will be dark. I will then start to sing or, as human beings call it, warble.

THE GARRET

For several months, Martin had been looking for an apartment to meet his not great, but very specific, demands. He had gradually adjusted his entire daily schedule to this search, even giving up his regular job. Several family matters, which some time earlier would have required his immediate attention, were so thoroughly neglected that it would have made no sense attending to them; so he readily left them to their fate. His search for an apartment had long since become an end in itself, a routine activity in which the object may change but the implementation remains the same. He would leave home in the morning, visit brokers, look at houses and building sites, and then come home in the evening; it was like going to a normal job. The urgency of the matter, however, was reduced by the fact that he was no longer aware of the need to have a better place to live, for, given his lack of time, he did not really make the most of his present apartment. He experienced something that so often happens in life: one looks for something and, while looking, forgets what one is looking for.

In one of the moments, however, in which he clearly recalled his original intention, he found exactly what he was looking for. He had walked along a completely destroyed street, hunting for an address he had obtained from an agency. Upon reaching the house, he saw that it was nothing more than a ruin, a skeleton with a few upright concrete pillars and steel supports—which, however, had maintained their original length only in the center of the former building —and a few cross-girths which held these supports together. The skeleton was incomplete, the flesh was missing altogether. Thus, one could not call it a house in the true sense of the word. Martin telephoned the broker, told him what he had found, and asked him whether there had not been a mistake. But the broker said there was no mistake, this was the right address; the agency was handling only the air space, he would have to build his own home; after all, the rent, as he himself had to admit, was extremely low. Martin did admit it, and after mulling the matter over, he decided to rent the air space for the garret—indeed, despite all doubts expressed by a friend who was an architect. The skeleton was not strong enough, the friend said, and it was not safe to live on such an inadequate foundation. Martin said that nothing was safe. In response to the rejoinder that within the general state of unsafeness, one had the possibility of forestalling an avertable accident, Martin said nothing, for he was not interested in the architect's opinion.

In order to lay the floor, the basic construction (if one could apply that term to something hovering in the air) had to be shored up with long girders from the ground. This unusual sight often caused passersby to halt and express their utter lack of understanding in their faces and sometimes in words, as well. Otherwise, however, the construction work proceeded in a normal way. At first, it was difficult hoisting up the materials, but the problem was soon solved by the capable contractor, who seemed to know how to deal with projects that were not run of the mill. The home grew; first the floor, then the walls and ceilings, and finally the lightly sloping roof. Next came windows and doors. The apartment door led into empty space, and one entered from the top rung of a rope ladder, so that one had to leave the garret backward in order to gain a solid foothold.

The first of a series of incidents occurred when the moving truck came. Martin's large desk, which was hanging from a rope, began to sway, striking one of the steel supports. The desk—an heirloom, but still a serviceable item of furniture —was undamaged, but not the support, which shattered like a candy cane. The workers and passersby gaped spellbound at the garret. They probably expected it to drop like a ripe fruit from the skeleton. But nothing of the sort happened. The garret did not stir. The desk was hoisted up and pulled through the garret window, and the rest of the furniture was moved in without any problems.

Martin himself was frightened for an instant, but he maintained his composure, and when people congratulated him with the phrase, "Well, it went well again," he replied that he had never doubted that his garret would endure the loss of a support.

The next incident, less critical, but nevertheless similar, was something he accepted with true equanimity. What happened was that a young married couple came in order, as they put it, to visit him in his new residence. First, they wanted to take some photographs, to which end the woman was to stand in a casual pose on the rope ladder. But when everything was ready, and the man leaned against a steel support in order to keep his camera steady, a few hard pieces of concrete dropped from the cross-girths, almost knocking the camera out of his hands. He was so furious at this incident that he refused to snap the photograph. Instead, he called to his equally indignant wife to climb down; and they went away after the husband shouted at Martin, who had been watching the course of events from the window, that their friendship was to be considered a thing of the past. Martin was not at fault, but he felt it made no sense to mention this. He registered the termination of their friendship with a smile and pulled the rope ladder up with joyful composure. What a happy marriage, he thought to himself, in which the reactions of the spouses are so finely attuned to one another.

The first of the two long concrete pillars broke during a visit from Martin's aunt. She came one day, greeted him from the street, and said she had not brought a housewarming present since she had told herself (privately) that in such a home every new piece imperiled the balance and must therefore be viewed as ballast. Martin called to her that he found

THE COLLECTED STORIES OF WOLFGANG HILDESHEIMER

her consideration quite sensible, that this was why he did not serve anything to his guests, for an overfilled pantry was as dangerous as overfilled stomachs, although the overall weight would, of course, be more safely distributed once the guests had partaken of the food. After this introduction, he threw the rope ladder down to the old lady, but it slipped away from her, banging against one of the two pillars. The pillar crumbled like a dry lump of sand. The rotten concrete trickled down in small streams, and what had been a column just a few seconds ago was now a pile. The aunt hurried away without looking back. The rope ladder swung to and fro, but the garret remained, now on one concrete pillar and one steel support.

The pillar was shattered by Martin's friend Robert. He was the only one who had the nerve not only to enter the garret but also to spend time there despite the imminent danger. At first, to be sure, his casual air was feigned, but then he grew accustomed to the precarious situation, and he alluded to it one evening by asking whether the garret would collapse if the second pillar also fell. Martin, who had begun acting somewhat above it all during the past few weeks, smiled, telling him to try it and pressing a hammer into his hand. Robert climbed down and smashed the pillar with a medium-strength hammer blow. After that, he no longer had the nerve to climb back up, and Martin had to toss Robert's hat down to him after getting it from the closet when he foresaw what would happen. Robert put down the hammer, rubbed the concrete dust from his hands, donned his hat, and left.

That same night, Martin began to hammer away at the last

steel support and thus the only prop between his garret and the ground. It was not curiosity that impelled him, for he had long since believed that his garret did not rest on the rotten bearers that fate had arbitrarily left standing. He wanted to get rid of this final prop, which was only a delusion and visually downright ludicrous. He felt that now the garret would finally acquire an appearance of sublime security as though borne by invisible hands. He climbed down, placed his hands with calm assurance on the final support, and snapped it like a flower.

He had no time to realize his fatal error. The roof slumped, the walls collapsed, smashing the floor to smithereens. The demolished garret fell almost as one piece, burying Martin under dust and debris.

A MAJOR

ACQUISITION

One evening, I was sitting in the tavern, over (more precisely, behind) a mug of beer when an unusual-looking man sat down next to me and asked in a softly intimate voice whether I would like to buy a locomotive. Now it is rather easy selling me something, because I find it hard to say no; however, I felt that caution was warranted with a major purchase of this sort. Although I know little about locomotives, I inquired about the model, the construction year, and the piston gauge; I was trying to make the man think that he was dealing with an expert who had no intention of buying a pig in a poke. I have no idea whether I really made him think so; in any case, he readily supplied information, showing me pictures of the sides, the front, and the back of the item. The locomotive looked good, and I ordered it once we agreed on a price. For it was secondhand, and although, as we know, locomotives wear out very slowly, I was unwilling to pay the catalog price.

The locomotive was delivered that same night. Perhaps the

all-too-speedy delivery should have given me pause to think that there was something shady about the transaction; but unsuspecting as I was, this never dawned on me.

I couldn't put the locomotive in my home, the doorways weren't large enough, and besides, the house would probably have collapsed under the weight; so I put the locomotive in the garage, which is certainly the right place for a vehicle. Naturally, only half the length fitted inside, but the roof was high enough. I had once stored a barrage balloon here, but it had burst.

Soon after this acquisition, I received a visit from my cousin. This man is averse to any sort of speculation, any display of emotion; for him, only facts are facts. Nothing surprises him, he knows better, and can explain anything. In short, an unbearable person. We said hello to each other and, in order to bridge the embarrassing silence that followed, I began: "These marvelous autumn scents—"

"Withering potato tops," he countered, and actually he was right. I threw in the sponge for now and poured myself some of the cognac he had brought. It tasted soapy, and I told him as much. He said that this cognac, as I could see on the label, had been awarded first prizes at world's fairs in Liège and Barcelona, even getting the Gold Medal at St. Louis; therefore, it was good. After we drank several glasses in silence, he decided to spend the night in my house and went to move his car into the garage.

A few minutes later, he came back and said in a soft, quivering voice that there was a huge express locomotive in my garage.

"I know," I said quietly, sipping my cognac, "I bought it just recently."

In reply to his timid question as to whether I often drove in it, I said no, not often; but a few nights ago, a nearby farmer's wife had been about to have a blessed event, and I had driven her to the city hospital. She had given birth to twins that same night, but that probably didn't have anything to do with the locomotive ride.

Incidentally, all this was made up; but on such occasions, I cannot resist embroidering a little on the truth. I don't know whether he believed me; he silently registered everything, and it was obvious that he no longer felt very comfortable here. He became monosyllabic, drank another glass of cognac, and then took his leave. I have never seen him again.

A short time later, when the newspapers reported that the French National Railroad had lost a locomotive (it had vanished from the face of the earth, or rather, the switchyard, one evening), I naturally realized that I had been the victim of a fraudulent transaction. When I saw the seller in the village tavern a short time later, I acted cool and reserved. On this occasion, he tried to sell me a crane, but I did not wish to have any more dealings with him. Besides, what am I going to do with a crane?

I CARRY AN OWL

TO ATHENS

One evening a year ago, I stood on the Acropolis and, with a sense of deep fulfillment, I released an owl that I had carried to Athens.

My decision to do so had taken shape one night when I couldn't sleep. In such dark hours, I make decisions that I then immediately carry out, circumstances at all permitting. This new and so far perhaps boldest decision could not be put into effect all that easily, but its realization could be prepared right away. I dressed and went off to see my bird dealer. His shop is closed at night, needless to say; regular patrons use a concealed night bell. I rang and was soon standing among cloth-draped cages in the nocturnal dimness of the bird shop. The owner asked me what I would like.

"An owl, please," I said.

"Aha," he said, winking, as if relishing the shrewd expertise of his client. "You're a connoisseur. Most customers make the mistake of selecting an owl in daylight. Should I gift-wrap it?"

"No. It's for me. I'd like to carry it to Athens."

"To Athens—aha!" The bird dealer slowly rubbed his chin with his thumb and forefinger, making the stubble crunch. He said, "Well, then I'd recommend a little owlet. I'm afraid that long-eared owls or barn owls would not be up to the vicissitudes of a lengthy journey. A little owlet, on the other hand, is tough, and its size is more manageable—"

"Carry an owlet to Athens?" I said slowly, testing the idea with quiet skepticism. The very rhythm did not appeal to me.

"The same family," the owner said. I held my tongue. "Nocturnal birds of prey," he added, spurred by the stubbornness of my silence. He was obviously unfamiliar with the nature of my qualms.

Some of my readers may have possibly experienced a similar dilemma and will therefore understand my doubts. In any case, I must confess, common sense won out over philological nit-picking: I bought the owlet. It did not seem worth running the risk of having an owl die shortly before I reached my destination, merely for the sake of all too pedantically refuting an ancient and utterly absurd presumption. Above all, I did not wish to violate the owl's soul by making its bearer the victim of a classical association. Man knows that God created him in His image, and he often has a hard time bearing this burden. But simile and similitude are alien to an animal, and, in my opinion, its animal dignity is enhanced by its ignorance of even the simplest fable about itself. Such were my musings as I walked home through the silent streets, loaded down with the owlet in a brass cage and a large package of Hartz's owl seed. For my thoughts about essence and being, about man and animals, come to me—if at all—within that dark, suggestive boundary between night and morning, at which hour even a little owlet transcends its earthly shape. I was carrying a symbol in my cage, as it were: the Animal *an sich.*

On the other hand, my sense of philological responsibility aroused a malaise, which I vainly tried to escape. What I was carrying in the cage was and would always be a little owlet, a bird evoking entirely different images than an owl. While any nonzoologist might mistake it for a real owl, I would know until my dying day that I had carried a little owlet to Athens. In the gray of dawn, I peered at the sleeping bird, which had no inkling of my qualms or its legendary aura; why, the good, harmless creature didn't even sense that it was a little owlet and not an owl. I don't know why I was touched by this latter thought—perhaps, in such hours, I feel more tender stirrings, which bring me closer to creation. In any event, I resolved, come what may, to carry this creature to Athens.

And my resolve was rewarded. Upon consulting *The Encyclopedia of Zoology* in the morning, I learned that I had, in spite of myself, made the right choice with the little owlet. For, while the barn owl answers to the zoological name of *Strix flammea,* and the long-eared owl is called *Otis vulgaris* (which latter adjective is, I am convinced, unfairly borne by this attractive bird), the little owlet is known as *Athene noctua;* and, in viewing the illustration, I realized that this was indeed the bird of the ancient image. Here I had it, in black and white, and I need have no qualms about carrying its living likeness to Athens.

THE COLLECTED STORIES OF WOLFGANG HILDESHEIMER

A few days later, I boarded the Orient Express. Sharing my compartment was a gentleman whose exterior bespoke the scholar. He was evidently traveling to Athens, albeit, of course, on a different mission. With restrained curiosity, he watched me stowing the cage on the baggage rack; and while I sat down and pulled my Pausanias from my pocket, his eyes remained glued to the bird, which slept quietly on its perch.

"An owl," I confirmed, without looking up from my book, feeling a profound peace of mind, a release from all doubts.

"A little owlet," he said.

"As you like," I said, looking up from my book after all. "In any case, this bird suits my purpose to a T."

"Are you by any chance," the gentleman asked with a lurking expression, "carrying this bird to Athens?"

"That is indeed my intention."

Now, the gentleman smiled. Inserting a mark into his book, he closed it, put it aside, and made himself comfortable in his corner, as if preparing for a long discussion of an interesting issue.

"My young friend," he commenced, "you have failed to read your Aristophanes carefully or else you have misunderstood him!" At this point, he paused as if to leave his demolished victim a choice between those two alternatives. But I did not choose—the charges were false; instead, I casually replied before he had a chance to continue: "I know, I know. It is considered the epitome of superfluousness to carry owls to Athens. I am familiar with this attitude. Nevertheless, as you can see, I am carrying such a bird to Athens."

"You mean a little owlet," the scholar said, a bit sharply,

82

it seemed, as though personally resenting my departure from the custom of taking Athena's bird, whether a little owlet or a real owl, to Athens.

Casually, almost indolently, I played my trump: "Athena's owl, as we know, was a little owlet. The translation of the word *glaukoopis* as "owl-eyed" is a philological inaccuracy, which I feel called upon to eradicate." I thereby deprived him of any possibility of retorting.

Nor did the gentleman retort. He was clearly a philologist, and his share of the traditional guilt left him speechless. He resumed reading, and from that point on (we were already passing the train station at Grosshesselohe), he acted as if the little owlet did not exist. He did not vouchsafe it a word, or even a glance, and I must be grateful to him for that, since the bird did a few things that, retrospectively, may not be worth mentioning, but that may have been viewed as troublesome if not unsuitable in the presence of so many travelers.

Now for some brief advice for those who, inspired by my example, have made up their minds to follow it: owls not being included in the list of declarable objects, one can resolutely challenge any duty demands made by customs officials. Cages, in contrast, are not duty-free, if they come fresh from the factory; however, a cage tenanted by a little owlet is soon no longer new. Gratuities are recommended. But do not count on sympathy from the train personnel, which is always changing; so if you do not know the tongue and body language of the countries you travel through, you will be unable to defend yourself effectively. On the whole, transporting an owl to Athens, admittedly, involves minor trouble, but it would be mendacious of me to deny that it is worth this trouble. Anyone who hopes for similar fulfillment from such actions as pouring water into the Thames or locking the stable door after the horse has been stolen will, I fear, be bitterly disappointed. Granted, the lack of ideal and material expenditures for these last-mentioned actions is attractive, and one is tempted to perform them, but the slight advantage of their simplicity is profusely made up for by the deep satisfaction one feels upon truly achieving one's goal.

For when I began climbing toward the Acropolis with my owl cage on the evening of my first day in Athens, I was overcome by a feeling of fervent contentment. I was performing an action that, unlike so many of today's experiments, was not aimed at refuting the theses of yesterday's teachers and do-gooders; rather, the point was to confirm their theses. I was convincing myself how useless it is to carry owls to Athens, not because there are so many there—neither I nor any Athenian I know of has ever seen a single owl in that city! No, the action was useless because owls are as useless there as they ultimately are here. Thus, my bliss will be understood by anyone who, like me, prefers doing things whose conception reveals from the very start that they will lead to nothing, so that seeing them through is a pure and blissful end in itself.

I bought my ticket, walked through the Propylaea, and halted in front of the Parthenon. With trembling fingers, I opened the cage. It was a grand moment. The owl rose into the air and fluttered away, to the pediment of the temple, where it perched for a while.

A classical sight! Against the blue night of the Attic sky,

which brought out the white of the marble, making it look spectrally beautiful, like porous velvet, my little owlet loomed forth, both a living creature and a symbol. I and no one else had carried it to Athens!

"Look, Selma," I heard a man next to me say, "that confirms the old saying that it's no use carrying owls to Athens. They even perch on the Parthenon."

"It's a little owlet," the woman replied.

The man held his tongue, probably embarrassed. He was most likely a humanist too, and his humanism, as is often the case, had developed at the expense of his zoology. However, the man could be helped. I turned to the two of them, easily recognizing a pair of honeymooners, and said, "It is a little owlet, the true bird of the goddess Pallas Athena. Today, most people still do not know this. But they soon will!"

With these self-confident words, I walked away, certain of their effect. I had helped a newlywed couple attain a more perfect image of classical reality or at least planted the seed of a correction.

I sold the cage to a scrap-metal dealer and began my trip home the next day. I am a very busy man and must budget my time very carefully. Self-discipline prohibits my extending at will such escapades from my everyday routine.

A few weeks later, the little owlet returned to my bird dealer. When a nocturnal bird of prey is tamed, it becomes deeply devoted to its master, a peculiarity that must certainly be counted among the zoological oddities. Nature is full of marvelous mysteries, and it frequently takes only a fluke to fathom one of them.

THE LIGHT GRAY
SPRING COAT

T wo months ago—we were just having breakfast —I received a letter from my cousin Eduard. My cousin Eduard left the house one spring evening twelve years ago, claiming he wanted to drop a letter in the mailbox, and never returned. No one had heard from him since. The letter came from Sidney, Australia. I opened it and read:

> Dear Paul,
>
> Could you send me my light gray spring coat? I can use it since it often gets severely cold here, especially at night. There is a *Pocket Manual for Mushroom Gathering* in the left-hand pocket. You can take it out and keep it. There are no edible mushrooms here. Many thanks in advance.
>
> Your cousin Eduard

I said to my wife, "I've received a letter from my cousin Eduard in Australia." She was just inserting the immersion heater into the flower vase in order to boil some eggs. She asked, "Really? What does he write?"

"He needs his light gray coat, and there are no edible mushrooms in Australia."

"Well, then he ought to eat something else," she said.

"You're right," I said.

Later, the piano tuner came. He was a somewhat timid and absentminded man, even a bit unsophisticated, but he was very nice and, naturally, very musical. He not only tuned pianos, he also repaired string instruments and gave recorder lessons. His name was Kolhaas. As I got up from the table, I could already hear him striking chords in the next room.

I saw the light gray coat hanging in the closet. My wife had obviously brought it down from the attic. I was surprised, for normally my wife does something only after it no longer matters whether it gets done or not. I wrapped the coat up carefully, took the package to the post office, and mailed it. It was only then that I realized I had forgotten to take out the mushroom book. But I am no mushroom gatherer.

I went for a short stroll, and when I came home, the piano tuner and my wife were wandering through the house, peering in the closets and under the tables.

"Can I help?" I asked.

"We're looking for Mr. Kolhaas's coat," my wife said.

"Oh," I said, realizing my error, "I've just sent it to Australia."

"Why Australia?" my wife asked.

"By mistake," I said.

"Well, then I won't intrude any longer," said Mr. Kolhaas, somewhat embarrassed, if not particularly surprised. He was about to excuse himself, but I said, "Wait, I'll give you my cousin's coat in exchange."

I went up to the attic, where I found my cousin's light gray coat in a dusty trunk. It was somewhat wrinkled—after all, it had been lying in the trunk for twelve years—but it was still in good condition.

My wife ironed it a little, while I sipped a glass of sherry with Mr. Kolhaas, and he told me about a few pianos he had tuned. Then he put on the coat, took his leave, and left.

A few days later, we received a package. It contained flat mushrooms, about two pounds. Two letters were lying on the mushrooms. I opened the first letter and read:

> Dear Mr. Holle [that is my name],
>
> Since you were kind enough to place a *Pocket Manual for Mushroom Gatherers* in my pocket, I would like to express my gratitude by sending you the results of my first mushroom gathering; I hope they are tasty. I also found a letter in the other pocket, which you probably left there accidentally. I herewith send it back to you.
>
> Truly yours,
> A. M. Kolhaas

The letter in question was probably the one my cousin had wanted to drop in the mailbox. He had clearly forgotten it at

home along with the coat. It was addressed to Bernhard
Haase, who, as I recalled, had been a friend of my cousin's.
I opened the envelope. A theater ticket and a note fell out.
The note said:

Dear Bernhard,

I am sending you a ticket for *Tannhäuser* for next Mon-
day, which I will not be using since I would like to go
out of town in order to unwind a little. Perhaps you feel
like going to the opera. Schmidt-Hohlweg is singing
Elizabeth. You are always so excited about her high G
sharps.

Best wishes,
Eduard

We had mushrooms for lunch. "I found the mushrooms on
the table. Where do they come from?" my wife asked.
"Mr. Kolhaas sent them."
"How nice of him. He shouldn't have."
"No," I said, "but it is very nice of him."
"I hope they're not poisonous. Incidentally, I also found
an opera ticket. What are they playing?"
"The ticket you've found," I said, "is for a performance
of *Tannhäuser*, but it was given twelve years ago!"
"Oh, well," said my wife, "I wouldn't have cared to go to
Tannhäuser anyway."
Today, another letter from Eduard arrived, asking me to
send him a tenor recorder. Inside the coat (which, strangely
enough, had grown longer, unless he himself had gotten

shorter), he had found a book on how to play the recorder, and he was planning to make use of it. But recorders were not available in Australia.

"Another letter from Eduard," I said to my wife. She was just taking the coffee mill apart, and she asked:

"What does he write?"

"He says there are no recorders in Australia."

"Well, then he should play a different instrument," she said.

"I think so too," I said.

My wife is refreshingly and disarmingly matter-of-fact. Her replies are straightforward but thorough.

I ORIENT MYSELF

One evening, about a year ago, I was visited by my uncle. He brought me two paintings that he said he had gotten for a good price at an auction. They were two large, heavy, genuine oil paintings on canvas with a dense impasto, in thick, gilded frames. Both pictures showed high mountain landscapes with snowy peaks, Alpine dairy farms, and home-coming woodcutters. The only essential difference was that one landscape shone in the light of the setting sun, while a storm was brewing over the other. Upon seeing them, I instantly realized that their titles would have to be *Alpenglow* and *Before the Storm*.

My uncle suggested that I hang the paintings right away. I could think of no excuse not to do so, and I hung them while he watched. "By the way, the titles are *Alpenglow* and *Before the Storm*," he commented.

"Oh, right," I said, "I was just about to ask you what the titles are."

Later, I opened a bottle of port wine, and we conversed. As we were sipping our second glass, Roeder showed up. Roeder, a friend of mine, is a painter in the modern direction, and I had just acquired a painting of his several days earlier. His visit was inconvenient, since, for some reason or other, I still had not hung up his painting, and now the two large landscapes were hanging there instead.

"Well, look at that," he said in a tone of quizzical surprise after greeting us both and walking over to the unfortunate paintings. *"Alpenglow* and *Before the Storm."*

"Why, those are the titles," my uncle said, amazed.

Trying to eye Roeder meaningfully, I explained to him that I had just received the pictures as presents from my uncle. But Roeder did not seem interested in dealing with this. He kept murmuring, "Very nice, very nice," with an absent-minded expression, and I had the feeling that roguish thoughts were operating behind that look. I found his conduct utterly tactless and I was therefore glad when he shortly took his leave. At the door, he gave me a friendly pat on the back. But this was not like him. I felt very uncomfortable, and for the rest of the evening my back remained burdened by that pat.

My uncle stayed, however, until the bottle was empty. When he left, I breathed a sigh of relief: the moment had come to take down the landscapes and hang up Roeder's abstraction. But I suddenly felt dispirited and strangely paralyzed. It may have been the aftereffect of the visit, or perhaps the wine had tired me. Port makes one lazy. In any case, climbing the ladder and changing the paintings seemed like a tremendous enterprise. I refrained.

The next morning, a huge crate was delivered to me. I had just taken out my tools to exchange the paintings. But I now used them to open the crate. A letter lay on top. It was from Roeder and it said:

Dear Robert,

Herewith a few objects that I assume will be to your taste.

Best wishes,
Roeder

Expecting something unpleasant, I began to unwrap. Out came, first, a porcelain vase, swathed in excelsior, depicting a crane with parti-colored plumage and a wide-open bill for inserting flower stems. Next to it, between layers of tissue paper, was a bouquet of artificial roses and a table lamp consisting of a nude female figure in cast iron, shouldering a light bulb socket and a wire shade covered with green silk in pleats and ruffles.

At the sight of these objects, my mood darkened. They did not make me think that Roeder earnestly believed my taste had suddenly changed, but I felt he had gone too far in his malicious, childish, deliberate misunderstanding. What was I supposed to do with these things in my two-room apartment? I had no attic or lumber room.

I was still brooding about the lack of taste shown by this prank when Sylvia arrived. Sylvia is impulsive and always tends to follow her momentary whims unconditionally. She often goes too far, as she did now. Her clear mind must have grasped the situation instantly. But instead of siding with me, she acted as if the only problem was to display several new acquisitions favorably. Not saying a word, she got moving. Taking a light bulb from a drawer, she screwed it into the lamp, which she carried into my bedroom. In a loving, feminine way, she arranged the artificial flowers in the vase, placing it on a bookshelf between the paintings, and, stepping back a few paces, she studied the effect. Then she sat down next to me and stroked my cheek.

Annoyed, I turned to her and said: "Listen, Sylvia, this is all a terrible misunderstanding, why it's almost a conspiracy. My uncle gave me these paintings last night. I shouldn't have hung them, but unfortunately, I did. Then Roeder arrived and saw the paintings. Next—"

She broke in, saying, "Why apologize? It makes no difference how you acquired these things. Now they belong to you."

The drift of these words was puzzling at the time, but the course of events soon made them clearer to me. Sometimes, I think she said, "Now they belong *with* you." In any case, that must have been what she meant.

Upon leaving, she said good-bye as though to a patient whom one does not wish to deprive of faith in his improvement. She looked into my eyes as if trying to inspire me with courage, stroked my cheek once again, turned abruptly away, and was gone.

But she returned that very same afternoon, bringing along her friend Renate. Renate went straight to my bedroom and began hammering. Meanwhile, Sylvia unpacked a number of lace doilies, saying she wanted to place them on the arms of the easy chairs, which was probably in keeping with my taste. Besides, they protected the slipcovers. I was so furious that I could not get a word out. Dumbstruck, I watched her arranging the doilies, smoothing them, pinning them down. Then she dragged me into the bedroom, where Renate had just set up a huge Black Forest cuckoo clock.

That did it. In a rage, I tried to pull the thing off the wall, but it was attached by means of two steel hooks, and when I yanked on it, the cuckoo shot out and angrily shrieked in my face six times. "Oh, it's six o'clock," said Renate, "we have to go."

Saying good-bye, which I registered virtually petrified, Sylvia promised to make me a couple of nice cross-stitch tablecloths. Then the two women quickly kissed me and hurried down the stairs, laughing. Their mirth echoed in my ears for a long while, as though a rival were laughing backstage after the curtain has fallen.

The cross-stitch tablecloths arrived two days later, and there was more. An architect friend named Mons had dropped by the evening before. He said that Roeder had told him about my new acquisitions and he had come to have a look. I tried (this time in a nervous agitation to which I gave full vent) to explain that it was all a nasty mistake. But he had merely peered at me with the earnest air of a diagnostician, as if attempting to find further symptoms of an incipient illness in my facial expressions. This only intensified my agitation, and when he shook hands with me upon leaving and said, "Good night, old boy," I furiously slammed the door behind him.

And now, accompanied by a card from him, came a huge, ivory-colored, high-gloss room divider with shelves looming in various directions on various levels. I immediately knew that it was supposed to hold cacti. The cacti, of various shapes and sizes, came that very same day, along with an illustrated pamphlet titled *The Joys of Cactus Growing*. With a composure that astonished me, I arranged the cactuses on the shelves and placed the pamphlet on my night table.

The night passed in fits and starts. The cuckoo awoke me several times. When I switched the lamp on, I saw the bronze woman; I could barely stand the sight, and, to take my mind off her, I picked up *The Joys of Cactus Growing* from the night table, but could not (yet) get excited about the contents, so I put the pamphlet down again and switched off the lamp. I nurtured unfriendly thoughts about my uncle, about Roeder, Sylvia, and the whole lot of them. Absorbed in these thoughts, I fell asleep, until the cuckoo woke me up again.

Several times that same week, I caught myself arranging the artificial flowers in the vase or smoothing out a lace doily on the arm of an easy chair; and when the crate with the bowls and the twisted candelabra arrived, I looked forward to each piece as I unpacked them. I did not even notice who had sent them to me.

The summer came. Sylvia was out of town, and so the

regular shipments of cross-stitch tablecloths and sofa cushions stopped; instead, she sent me multicolored picture postcards depicting various tourist attractions. I arranged them in an album.

One evening, Renate visited me, bringing an album of records. She insisted that I play something immediately. First, we put on a fantasia entitled *From Weber's Magic Forest,* next *The Most Beautiful Choruses from Wagner's Operas,* and, in conclusion, the finale from Beethoven's Fifth Symphony. Then she left. When she was gone, I played the ballet music from *Rosamunde* and went to bed. The cuckoo clock struck twelve. I had begun to orient myself by it.

I tried to rebel one more time; it was the day when Herr von Stamitz, who was now engaged to Sylvia, sent me the grained walnut bookcase and the mock-up books. Today, it is no longer clear to me why I so utterly lost my temper on this occasion rather than another, given the irreproachable craftsmanship of the thing. I recall that I scurried around my apartment as if in a cage. I tried to pull the doilies off the armchairs: I had forgotten that I had sewn them on in the meantime. I attempted to rip up a few cross-stitch tablecloths with my teeth, but the material was too hard, they were made of good, tough rustic linen. Sylvia had always despised inferior material. The only thing that broke was an expensive African sculpture, one of the few mementos of the period before my uncle's visit. I had to laugh at this exemplary accident, and my anger waned. Calmly I got to work, arranging the book spines in the walnut case and securing them at either end. In so doing, I read the names Gibbons, Macaulay,

Mommsen, and Ranke. It was a selection for historians. I have always been interested in history.

That night, I dreamed I was wandering through empty halls with only an occasional piece of utilitarian furniture. I sat down on a steel footstool. Instantly, upholstered backs and arms grew out of it with repp and velvet cushions. Crystal chandeliers sank down from the ceiling. Women in flowing gowns, their hair rolled up in curlers over their ears, dragged heavy, gilt-edged volumes over, which they opened in front of me. The pages were pasted up with engravings and photographs sporting captions such as "Franz Liszt with Friends," or "Gloaming on Lake Lomond," or "Hiroshima My Love." I woke up when the grandfather clock in the living room struck three. I flicked on the night-table lamp, and there was the bronze figure standing before me, so terribly present, I flicked the lamp off again, but the cuckoo called three times —it was obviously slow—I switched the lamp on again and threw *The Joys of Cactus Growing* at the cuckoo. It missed. I threw the Rosenthal porcelain stag, but hit the risqué copperplate print *La surprise,* which hung next to the cuckoo clock. The glass shattered, and I calmed down. The crisis was over.

Thus did my apartment slowly grow. I had fewer and fewer visitors, for it was now somewhat difficult threading one's way through the furniture in order to reach something to sit on; and even if you did reach it, you could not sit down anyway because the chairs were covered with framed engravings, all kinds of utensils, and even an occasional piece that had won some prize for being so nobly down to earth.

My uncle visited me one more time, but I could not see him,

for I was lying in bed, and he could not find a way to get to me. He had brought me a painting, which, this time, as he called to me, depicted something modern, and I asked him to place it on one of the teakwood tables of which there had to be several in the hallway. He called back that the tables were already covered with all sorts of ceramic vessels—things, incidentally, of obvious artistic quality. I did not reply and I therefore cannot tell whether my uncle left the painting here or took it along again, for I have been lying in bed ever since. My uncle was my last visitor.

I cannot get up anymore, for even if I do find my way through the bedroom, I will get lost in the living room. I lie here, dozing, looking at postcards or heliogravures, or else, on the phonograph next to my bed I play a serenade of Schubert's or his "Ave Maria" sung by a Black singer. She has such a lovely, calming voice. I also sometimes read *The Joys of Cactus Growing,* from which I have learned, say, that cacti bloom. Perhaps one of mine has bloomed, but I cannot tell, for, as I have said, I no longer go into my living room.

I can sleep again now, for one night I hit the cuckoo with a Swedish glass vase just as the cuckoo was about to slip back in. The grandfather clock in the living room stopped long ago, but I cannot get to it in order to wind it up. Nor do I wish to; it would make no sense.

THE STUDIO PARTY

For some time, a rowdy party has been going on in the studio next door. I have gotten used to it, and the noise no longer bothers me. But sometimes, there are high points, things get frantic, and I feel impelled to complain to my landlord. After I had done so several times, he came one evening to see for himself. But, as is often the case, a lull had set in, and so my landlord rejected my complaint as unjustified. I had hoped I might let him see for himself how untenable the situation was: to this purpose, I opened the wardrobe and let him peek through a crack in the wall. You see, behind the wardrobe there is a hole the size of a porthole in a tourist-class cabin. He peered through for a while, but all he emitted after climbing back out of the closet was a grunt indicating he had registered something. Then he left, and, a few hours later, when the party was going full blast again, I peeked through the hole and saw that my landlord was an eager participant in the studio party.

A bit upset, I paced up and down my living room; but, as always on such occasions, my shuttling was made difficult by the rigid and immovable arrangement of the objects. At the slightest bump, the lead crystal on the shelves tinkles, the teakwood table wobbles even though I constantly wedge cigarette packs under its feet, and the light-footed Finnish vase topples over at the slightest quiver as if that were its function. I finally halted in front of the print of Picasso's *Blue Youth*. How wonderful, I thought, these faithful replicas are, how cunning the modern reproduction technique. After such annoyances, this is one of several good ways to focus my mind on something else; and, soothed, if not purged, I then go to the icebox to sip a glass of cold peppermint tea, an excellent beverage for such mental states; every single sip confirms that I have once again carried the day in my struggle against rebellion. I then usually, if not always, play a game of solitaire.

For in this apartment, which I have called my own for a long time now, the customs do not seem to have been changed by my moving in. They cling to the furnishings and decorations. The atmosphere dictates the actions of the tenants, and I often feel as if I ought to go to some normal office. However, the implementation of this idea is frustrated by my lack of decisiveness; besides, I do not know what kind of office it would be. Still, don't count your chickens before they are hatched—as I often tell myself, albeit not quite appropriately.

I peer through the hole less and less often. I have noticed that the makeup of the party keeps changing. Guests who were there at the beginning have now left, others have taken their place. Some of them actually seem to have been cloned, for example, the poet Benrath, whom I constantly think I see in two different spots at once: a bizarre, almost tendentious optical illusion. I notice that Gerda Stoehr has dyed her hair —perhaps with pigments that once belonged to me; I recognize the actress Halldorff, whom I last saw eight years ago as Mary Stuart (apropos, an unforgettable experience!) Frau von Hergenrath has left (perhaps she has died in the meantime?). But the glazier—yes, he is still there, and has been all along.

He was there the afternoon the studio still belonged to me, that memorable afternoon when I wanted to start painting again after a long dry spell. He was replacing a few broken windowpanes, hammering away softly. My wife was in the next room, asleep; it was raining outside; I can still feel the mood. Sensing that I was on the right track after weeks of searching for inspiration, I joyously blended the colors, relishing the spicy fragrance of the emulsions.

The glazier was still glazing, in silence. He won't be in the way, I thought to myself. But when I placed the canvas on the easel, he said, "I paint too."

"Really," I said coolly. Perhaps I also said, "Oh"; in any case, my comment was monosyllabic.

"Yes," he went on nevertheless, encouraged. "Mountain motifs in watercolors. But not as modern as these things, where you can't tell which way is up. I paint what I see." He spoke with the aggressive authority of the amateur. "Do you know the landscape painter Linnertsrieder? I paint like him."

I said I did not know this landscape painter and resolved to wait until the glazier left before I got to work. For I knew this narrow mood ridge: if I gave free rein to my irritability, the conception of my painting would instantly totter. I sat down in an armchair, lit a cigarette, and tried to nudge along the coming creative act, gingerly, gingerly, so as not to injure it.

But before the glazier was done with his work, Frau von Hergenrath arrived. I stopped nudging and suppressed a sigh of resignation. I had to keep calm: she was a patron of the arts, and made substantial contributions to my livelihood. For art goes a-begging, as everyone who knows nothing about it will keep assuring you,

"I have come," the good lady said, "to see how you are." She looked around as if seeking me amidst the paintings. "I hear you are going through a dry spell."

I was really in no mood to discuss the whims of my muse with Frau von Hergenrath. I therefore assured her that the very opposite was the case, that I was in full possession of my creative powers, and I made a lively gesture toward the surrounding paintings as witnesses. They were old, and Frau von Hergenrath had seen them all several times, but I could bank on her defective memory. Indeed, she did not recognize the paintings and she tackled them with fresh, irrelevant criticism, several times stating the opposite of what I recalled her early opinion to be. I listened to her somewhat tormented, as is my wont on such occasions. But at least the glazier had lapsed into silence. Holding his tongue, he resumed his hammering. I noticed that the rain had stopped. Time stood still.

The sleepy afternoon took an abrupt turn when Engelhardt burst into the room, Engelhardt, the unbearable companion, with his deadly heartiness, whom one cannot resent, however, for, like ripe Camembert, he is soft beneath his unpleasant crust, which ultimately makes him even more unbearable. The last straw: I flinched at the thought of the slap he would promptly aim at my back. He kissed Frau von Hergenrath's hand, then jumped on me, and slapped. Next, he shouted, something with the words "old boy" and asked, "How's tricks?"

"So, so," I said. I scarcely vary the answer to such questions from case to case. I have never succeeded in finding a response that is both terse and exhaustive, nor was it necessary, for the persons asking this question always seemed satisfied with these vague words.

"I see," this person went on, joining Frau von Hergenrath in viewing a few extremely weak examples of my early work, "the muse never stops kissing you. We'll have to drink to that." He produced a bottle of cognac from his coat pocket. He was truly enviable in his ability (his only goal in life) to bring about so-called high spirits. "A talented devil, eh?" he asked Frau von Hergenrath. He meant me. I was busy getting glasses, so I could not see whether he thrust his elbow in her side, as was his wont.

Now, my wife joined us. She is always awoken by the sound of popping corks, even from far away; it works when kitchen alarm clocks fail. She walked toward us and greeted us with reserve. I had the feeling that she actually recognized no one but myself: it was always a little hard for her to find her bearings after a nap, but a few drinks helped her regain her —often highly individual—perspective. Engelhardt poured her a generous measure. He then wanted to fill Frau von Hergenrath's glass, but she placed her flat hand upon it, saying she never drank at this time of day. Her statement, naturally, contained a barb, aimed at me: any artist enjoying her patronage but pursuing nonartistic activities in broad daylight was to be investigated! However, Engelhardt did not catch this subtle dig. Applying his humorous art of persuasion, he managed to get her to accept a so-called "half a glass." This broke the ice, impelling her to flout her own principles, and thereafter, she did, as the phrase goes, ample justice to the cognac.

Unfortunately, I was unable to prevent Engelhardt from offering the glazier a drink. The latter had been hammering away senselessly although he must have completed his work long since. He liked it here. At Engelhardt's invitation, he came over to the table, saying, "Don't mind if I do," and— there is no other way of phrasing it—he tossed the liquid down his throat. "I paint too," he thereupon said to Engelhardt, as if justifying his acceptance in our group. "Who doesn't paint?" Engelhardt asked foolishly, but the glazier did not know how to respond, and so he involved my wife in an—admittedly one-sided—conversation on art.

As we sat there, the door opened, and a pair of strangers, presumably a married couple, came in. Since the drink made my wife forget her duties as a hostess, I stood up and greeted the newcomers as cordially as I might under the circumstances. The man introduced himself (I did not catch his name; I have never caught any name at any introduction, for every name catches me off guard) and said he had been recommended to me by Hébertin in Paris. "Aha, Hébertin," I said, nodding, as if visualizing the period I had spent with him; yet I had never heard of the man. I presented the couple to my wife and the others, mumbling a few vowels that I thought I had heard in their name, and stressing the recommendation from Hébertin, but he did not seem to ring a bell in anyone's mind. My wife brought some more glasses, Engelhardt produced a second bottle from a different coat pocket, and the couple were already part of the festivities.

Somehow, the situation had gotten out of control. First of all, I was unnerved by the sight of this glazier; he had put his hand on Frau von Hergenrath's arm and was telling her that he painted what he saw, but she was not listening, she was warbling softly. Second, I had been seized with a feeling of helpless melancholy. My vision of the painting I was planning had crumbled; the Muse had fled with her face veiled, leaving nothing behind but a tantalizing scent of turpentine. I looked at the unknown couple. Both were smoking cigars. They seemed to feel at home. The woman was telling my wife that Hébertin had moved to Rue Marbeau and was still, alas, addicted to his old habit. Judging by the woman's facial expression, it must have been something worse than drugs.

Meanwhile, Engelhardt, the master of the situation, had rung up several people (he called this action: "drumming up") to tell them there was a party in my studio. He asked them to come and bring friends, relatives, and, above all, bottles with extremely potent contents. I had a very hard time preventing the glazier from following Engelhardt's example. I amiably slapped him on the back and explained that if too many people came, we would not get very much out of one another; for after all, the essence of any social gathering was "conversation." Surprisingly enough, my words struck home.

The first person to come was Gerda Stoehr, flanked by two elderly gentlemen, impeccable, with class, born protectors both of them. They peered about in amazement. But when their tousled protégée greeted my wife in baby talk, the two gentlemen exchanged smiles of acknowledgment, and the process of ice-breaking began, not stopping at anything or anyone.

And then the noisy swarm of guests burst in, each loaded with one or more bottles. I knew some of them, for instance, Vera Erbsam, my wife's intimate bosom friend, who had always made eyes at me until the day I told her that my father ran a bakery in Dobritzburg; ever since, she has always eyed me suspiciously. Still, she had come, bringing along a young man, whom I also knew casually, a legal assistant or junior lawyer, unless these are one and the same. He looked like someone's fiancé—presumably hers. There was also a pair of movie actors of enigmatic origins; their name was De Pollani, but it was probably not their real name, and they were probably not married either. I had once done the woman's portrait, on which occasion she had removed her sunglasses. I heard Engelhardt, who had taken over the role of host, address Madame De Pollani as "darling," thus expanding by yet another décolleté the panorama of worlds on whose soils he moved with complete aplomb.

I need not dwell on each guest individually. To do justice to the mood, it would suffice to say that even before nightfall the company became a single homogeneous mass in which sober newcomers kept submerging, instantly becoming parts of the whole. "Life should just be one long studio party," I heard a young colleague saying not far from me.

"Life *is* one long studio party," said the bearded man next to him. He was an art critic, famous for his pungent off-the-cuff aphorisms. It dawned on me that I had invited him to dinner for that evening, but he seemed to have reconciled himself to the altered situation. He stood there, smiling pensively into his glass and constantly tapping the point of his shoe on fat Schmitt-Holweg, who lay on the floor, colossal and drunk. He was a sculptor who carried his calling with painful relentlessness, to which he gave babbling expression, looking like something concocted by Rabelais in a drunken fit.

Shortly before midnight, I was squeezed to the wall with my face flat against it. A procession of bacchantes rolled past, making it impossible for me even to turn halfway and sit down on my own paintings. In this desperate situation, I discovered a hammer in the pocket of the man next to me. It was the glazier. I shouted, "May I, for one moment?" (although politeness was out of place here; for one could barely hear oneself think). I took the hammer from his pocket, and began to smash through the wall.

Since I could not swing back far behind me without endangering the guests, this labor was strenuous and progressed rather slowly. First, the plaster crumbled off in small flakes, then the cement loosened, dropping into sand and gravel and soon forming a mound at my feet. The gathering behind me seemed to have reached a climax, but I paid it no heed. From the opposite corner of the room, I heard a female voice singing an off-color ditty through the drunken racket. Under normal conditions, I would have been embarrassed because of Frau von Hergenrath; but now that I was about to slip out of the studio, I did not care. Incidentally, I soon realized that it was Frau von Hergenrath who was singing. Evidently, she had facets that I had never suspected since they probably needed to be somewhat unleashed in order to emerge fully.

The hole grew. After a while, I broke through to the other side and, with the aid of the light pouring through from my studio, I could survey the situation in my neighbors' bedroom. Their name was Giesslich, it probably still is, and they are still my neighbors in a certain sense. These were modern, but upright people, however, this latter quality has changed a bit—namely, toward the former quality—and I do not wish to deny my responsibility in the matter.

The two of them sat up in their beds, switched on the light, and greeted me, astonished, but not unfriendly; indeed, I must admit they displayed a certain tender indulgence such as artists seldom experience from their middle-class fellowmen, especially in such unusual situations. Perhaps, they had instantly become cognizant of their modernity upon awakening. I was so embarrassed that at first I greeted them perfunctorily and kept hammering until the aperture reached the size it still has today. I then asked somewhat clumsily, "May I come in?" and without waiting for an answer, I squeezed through.

After brushing the cement dust from my shoulders with my hand in order to keep my nocturnal emergence from seeming all too makeshift, I said, "Please excuse me for disturbing you at such a late hour, but I have come to invite you to a party which is taking place in my studio tonight." A pause. "It is a lot of fun."

The Giesslichs looked at one another, a reaction from which I was relieved to infer that they considered my invitation worthy of discussion. I wanted to go on speaking, but Herr Giesslich said, with what I felt was a somewhat saccharine smile, that he was grateful for the kind invitation, but that a couple of their age, although of a modern frame of mind, did not really fit in a group of people whose common task in life, namely art, gave them a common destiny, which they, the Giesslichs, did not really share.

On the contrary, I said, artists of all people have the quality of making any outsider feel instantly at home with them; besides, the party was made up of a varied mixture of guests, from aristocratic patronesses to simple working men. For the first time that night, I developed a tremendous eloquence, finally managing to arouse their interest in the party; indeed, by telling them that everyone was dressed very casually, I succeeded in persuading them not to bother changing, but to slip across in their night clothes. I had told them a lie, but I sensed a growing need to be alone at last.

They got out of their beds. Herr Giesslich was wearing a striped pajama, she had a nightgown on. He helped her into her dressing gown as into an evening coat and, already impatient, he hurried up and down while she combed her hair at the dresser mirror. I had truly managed to ignite their enthusiasm; naturally, I wondered which enticement had tipped the balance: The humanitarian qualities of the artists? Or the presence of aristocratic patrons? When I peer through the hole, however, I feel that it was probably the business about dressing casually, which is becoming more and more of a terrifying truth.

First, Herr Giesslich squeezed through the hole. He must have gotten a solid foothold on the other side, for he gallantly offered his wife his hand as though helping her up the high steps of a coach. I had to do my bit on my side, for Frau Giesslich's circumference was considerable, and, incidentally, still is. But she too had reached firm ground. I was alone.

With some expenditure of strength, I shoved the heavy wardrobe in front of the hole, where it still stands today. Now, things got much quieter, for the clothing in the wardrobe muffled the noise. Furthermore, the party itself had calmed down a bit, a more peaceful lull between two high points.

Exhausted, I dropped down on one of the two beds and tried to think about my situation, but I was too tired and could do no more than digest the immediate impressions; after all, I had a very strenuous evening behind me. From far away, I heard the whistle of a locomotive, and I still recall being glad that I could make out other sounds besides the fracas of the party next door (at that moment, it was reduced to a humming). Through the curtains, I saw that it was getting light out, day was dawning, a time when I, if awake, glide toward a lengthy row of images, memories, and dismal inklings. In between, I heard the crowing of a rooster, the only function of the feathered creature that gives it some claim to poetic processes, I thought to myself, noticing that, as so often in unfamiliar situations, my thoughts were becoming independent. At this point, I fell asleep. I woke up late in the afternoon. I peered through the hole. The party was still going full blast, and I knew it would go on forever.

THE VACATION

For some time now, Adrian had been waking up at dawn. Sleep left him like a dispersing fog, gently, but relentlessly, and there he was, transposed into the twilight of reality. Hard as he tried to flee back into this sleep, drift upward to grab a corner of the foggy cloud, he never succeeded. Wakefulness crept up his legs, tensing his body. Thus he lay there, while the threads of reality were bound together again in his consciousness, tying yesterday to today and making any escape impossible. He gave up. The gathering daylight brought the routine of daily tasks in which, it seemed to him, one so often was about to submerge.

These thoughts haunted him now, on the morning of a day filled with important appointments. He was torn from his pensiveness by the ringing of the telephone. At the same time, somebody knocked on his apartment door. Which first? The day thus began with a dilemma, thought Adrian, planning to open the door and ask the person to wait until he answered the ringing. But then he realized he was inadequately dressed. He closed his ears to the knocking and went to the telephone.

It was Mariella calling up from town to invite him to dinner. Adrian thanked her, saying he would love to come.

Then he explained to her why it was impossible for him to linger on the telephone as usual: he had overslept, besides someone was knocking at the door; and Adrian hung up. But the knocking had stopped. He went to the door and saw that it had only been the mailman. Adrian must have gotten up later than normal. His watch had stopped. He had, as so often nowadays, forgotten to wind it. He took the mail out of the box. It consisted of a four-page brochure asking him to buy some objects at greatly reduced prices, and a package, probably a book for him to review. Adrian had been expecting some urgent letters, but this was all right. He tossed the brochure into the wastebasket and inserted the book in the pocket of his coat in order to read it on the train. Then he went to the closet to dress carefully.

In order to get to the city, which Adrian visited once a week, he had to walk or bicycle the three miles to the nearest market village and then take a one-hour train ride. It was a very warm November morning. A hoar had settled at dawn, but the air was still redolent with the zest of late summer, and Adrian had decided to walk the three miles. But now that he was late, he took the bicycle instead. When he passed the village church, however, he looked at the steeple clock and saw that it was not later than usual, so he might just as well have walked. That was why he pedaled slowly; he wanted to enjoy the final warmth that the waning year had to offer. It was only upon reaching the station and learning he had missed the train that he remembered the church clock had stopped quite awhile ago, and that the works had been removed several months back.

The information panel told him that the next train would leave in one hour. He checked the bicycle at the storage shed and went into the tavern across the way.

While sitting here in the empty barroom, with his back toward the Dutch oven, sipping the gentian spirits he had ordered, Adrian was overcome with a feeling of peace and quiet such as he had not known for days—no, it seemed more like months. He stretched out in physical well-being as in a warm bath and looked at the November sun, which was shining through the tree skeletons into the tavern.

Suddenly, an unwelcome thought emerged. He tried to grab it—what was it?—and after a few minutes he had it: Mariella. He had forgotten the date and time of her dinner, or rather, he had once again not really listened. He would have to call her back, though not right now. He did not care to interrupt this well-being, this unexpected vacation. But he was wrought up now; peace and quiet would not return.

When he felt it was time, he stood up and went to the station. Neither travelers nor railroad officials were to be seen on the platform. Two boys were running along the tracks outside the station, trying to get a kite to rise. Otherwise, everything was silent. Two freight cars stood on the shunting track. They had always been standing there. The words HOME STATION KASSEL were written on them. How had they wound up here? thought Adrian.

He waited for a few minutes, then went to the ticket window and asked whether the 10:41 train was running. The man gazed silently at him for a moment and then said (his voice sounded sad but strict, and a bit glad to be giving unpleasant information) that this train never ran on weekdays, but only on Sundays. Today was Tuesday. Furthermore, it only ran during the summer, for it was an observation train. All this was indicated on the panel if the gentleman could read.

"Well, well, an observation train," said Adrian; and since, as so often in situations of minor despair, he felt like joking, he said that his observation faculties were not strongly developed. But the man had closed his window. The contact with the world of officialdom was broken off.

Adrian went to the information panel to find a train that also ran in the winter, and he did find one. The crossed hammers behind the departure time, 5:57 P.M., indicated that it also ran weekdays. That much he knew.

He went back to the tavern, with a sense of disquiet (for now all his appointments were voided), but also with a light heart, for he intended to get himself back into his vacation mood and artificially continue it. Explanations and apologies would come later. In case Mariella's dinner was scheduled for tonight, which was possible, of course, he would still arrive on time. For that was one dinner he must not miss. It was more important than anything else. He would call Mariella up. But not now, not right now.

He sat down in the same place in the barroom and ordered lunch from the proprietress. She was glad to see him again, for he had forgotten to pay for his drink. When asked what he would like to order, he pleasurably replied that he was so hungry he could devour an entire horse. The proprietress said they did not carry horses. Then, said Adrian, he would confine himself to what they did carry. They carried pork chops.

While waiting for his order, Adrian recalled the book in his coat pocket. He unwrapped it. The title was *On Sunny Trails.* He opened it morosely. The jacket said, "This collection of authentic nature poems will appeal to all readers whom the hustle and bustle of everyday life . . ." He put down the book.

When the proprietress brought him his lunch, he asked her whether they had a telephone here. They did not. He breathed a sigh of relief, but was unaware that he had breathed it.

Late afternoon found Adrian still in the tavern. The sky was overcast, and around the mountains, the clouds hinted at snow. The peaks were shrouded. Adrian had been sitting in the empty tavern and, in order to calm his growing malaise, he had drunk several glasses of gentian spirits. This had made him sleepy. After a great deal of soul-searching, he still could not resolve to spend an hour on the train during the late twilight. He had tried *On Sunny Trails* for a moment, but its wealth of poignancy had aroused his stolid aversion. So he had asked the proprietress to rent him a room, and when the afternoon train left the station, Adrian was fast asleep.

When he awoke the next day, deep snow lay everywhere. Everything around him was white, mild, and still. His peace and quiet had come back. He dressed and went downstairs. While serving him breakfast, the proprietress informed him that because of the sudden, unexpected snowfall, trains were not in service in this area. Adrian registered the news calmly and asked her to heat his room.

In the afternoon, he thought of calling the city from the station in order to explain his situation to his friends, especially Mariella; but after thinking about it, he decided not to. He should have done it yesterday, as an immediate and (he now admitted to himself) rather obvious reaction to this unusual merger of coincidence and carelessness. His appointments were all long voided now anyway, the dinner party might already have taken place. When he thought of people worrying about him, he almost felt pleasure. Remaining here for a while required no decision. If the trains were not running, then the streets were certainly not negotiable.

But the next day, he could not stop thinking about Mariella, he was haunted by the thought of her. He decided to call her up, and he waded through the snow to the station. Here, a few workers were removing the iron gate that separated the platform from the highway. Their work proceeded soundlessly in the deep snow, their breath steamed. The telephone booth, which had once been attached to the gate, was gone. Adrian pensively returned to the inn. He decided not to inquire about this circumstance.

Two days later, Adrian walked through the snowy village to do some shopping. He was struck by the lack of activity. When he subsequently imparted his observation to the proprietress, she said the village population had gone down during the past few months because there were fewer and fewer jobs. She too intended to leave soon.

What would it be like, Adrian wondered, living in a ghost village? The thought of such a strange, voluntary isolation aroused the kind of fantasies that he frequently liked to dwell on. Nevertheless, he decided—quite noncommittally—to check the information panel. He would reserve the decision to travel. And one day (it had gotten warmer and a thaw had come), he went over to the station. The information panel was gone. He knocked on the ticket window. No one opened. Worried, he walked through the open gate to the platform. Here, a few workers were pulling up the tracks.

"What are you doing there?" he called as if to prevent someone from carrying out an unreflected deed. Adrian now learned that the rail network was being shifted because of insufficient use of this line. And indeed, the station was desolate, part of the building had been torn down, the glass removed from the windows, which, black holes now, made it look like a ruin. The posters were ripped off, the many "prohibited" signs had been removed. Even the two freight cars had vanished. They had probably returned to their home in Kassel.

Adrian was scared. He dashed over to the storage shed to get his bicycle. It was still there, wet and dirty. He grabbed it and pedaled off without looking back; first, a few difficult miles on muddy dirt roads; then, on the other side of the former underpass (the tracks were already removed), he turned into the highway, toward the city, which he reached after several hours. His throat was parched, the sweat was running from his temples. He rode like a sleepwalker, heeding neither traffic lights nor pedestrians, making his way toward Mariella's home. He leaned the bicycle against the wall and rang her bell tempestuously. After a while, the door opened; it was Mariella herself.

"Mariella," he cried, but his voice was so toneless that it sounded like a sigh.

"The last one, as usual," she said with a smile and kissed him; "we've all been waiting for you. Incidentally, you look as though you need to freshen up a bit. But hurry! The meal is about to be served."

THE GRUEL ON

OUR STOVE

Gruel is on all our stoves. It would take many cooks to spoil it properly and thoroughly.

The first is the chubby-cheeked cook of our earliest years, and thus not a real cook, but a pastry chef. Today, the good man is still laboring under the illusion that saffron makes a cake yellow, an opinion with which one can no longer get very far in our time. However, our friend is as unteachable as we were in our childhood. Like a grandfather drowsing in a wing chair, he is preparing an aura of stubborn inaccessibility in a certain mild, restrained way; only, of course, if we speak of areas that he used to be able to call his own. Mute and reproachful, as if it were our fault that the centuries are waning, he points to the admittedly splendid, spic-and-span, copper-shining gugelhupf shapes in the kitchen of the Goethe House in Frankfurt. Well, much as one might wish to glean a spiritual reference from this mute rebuke, say, in the guise of an Eternal Truth (for after all, each of us has his bit of

Biedermeier in his blood and is bashfully and ardently attached to the days of cookie-baking, lamp-polishing menials who were ordered to keep their traps shut and stay out of sight), we nevertheless may appropriately remark that we live in a different era, which, after all, is ultimately the case. One must, however, frame this remark in solicitous words and strew them casually, like a pinch of spice on a successful dish: we do not wish to offend our good childhood-cook. But he does hear the wee discord in our mellifluous melody; and, with his confectionery-sugar-white hands, he makes a gesture of resignation as if he simply cannot help us. Nor, indeed, can he. The fact that he is the one who needs help should not be mentioned because of the great respect he is owed. He is amply punished for being trapped in his time, as we are for initially believing that this is a man who can spoil our gruel.

We are thus free to consult the second cook. This is the cook for the bishop of Mozambique. Our message reaches him in Äschwyl on Lake Gurten, where, after ten torrid tropical years, which have not left him unscathed. he is spending a well-deserved vacation of several months. Äschwyl is an orderly, doughty, crenellated town, which, having been put on the map of local history by the Battle of Sempach, has been hoarding its significance like a pretty treasure. It lies in the Swiss Jura Mountains, so our cook is Swiss, as is, incidentally, his employer, the bishop: a wise, thoroughly decent diabetic, who treats even the plainest, nakedest African child as his equal, thus being able to boast of more successful conversions than some starry-eyed, faith-glowing, cross-and-chain-swinging Capuchin padre, who has nothing but grim, destructive scorn or a blind eye, or both, for the variegated totem poles and taboo tokens. But this is neither here nor there.

The cook's name is either Kuno or Kaspar (one must make up one's mind) and he feels generally fine under the all-embracing, black-velvet pinions of his lord and shepherd. For a few good, cheering words are dropped for him, as well as a decent salary—not more, of course. You see, the bishop lives in strict adherence to dietary rules, and so his cook sometimes deeply regrets that he must serve the good cause rather than many good things. The bold plans of his youth, Hungarian paprika goulash and early Serbian onion shashlik, have, perforce, been buried in farina and rice pudding; and now, on unusually hot days, when, dressed only in a scant loincloth and headgear, he takes his afternoon siesta under a date tree, he dreams about a wild African dish, prepared in gigantic iron caldrons, a darkly iridescent sauce, brewed amidst cannibal invocations, to the rhythm of jungle drums, and personally spiced by the mask-glaring medicine man. Only he who has not been forced to bury a youthful dream will hold this debauchery against Kuno or Kaspar.

He comes. By bicycle, for he must enjoy his vacation, even in the guise of dandelions or meadow cress along the roadside. The two cooks greet each other amiably, nay, almost heartily. After all, they have the same propensities, they selected the same goal in life. Such things connect one. Furthermore, both men have harmonious temperaments, meek, humble natures, they are not virtuosi engaged in blazing rivalry or smoldering competition. Mozambique may be almost as remote as the land of our childhood, but it lies in a different direction; these cooks do not poach on each other's preserves. Pot-and-pan realms are staked off, and seas, deserts, decades lie between them. Neither man knew about the other until now. We, on the other hand, know only that the first one cannot spoil any gruel. Can the second one? We do not wish to jump the gun: in this account, chronology is of the essence.

Kuno (let us stick to this name, for simplicity's sake) lifts the lid and peers into the pot. He sinks his finger knuckle-deep in the milky farina, keeps it there (his extremities are accustomed to heat), closes his eyes, and counts to three. Then he withdraws his finger from the pot and licks it. He pauses for effect (even a preparer of light diets enjoys the opportunity to put on little airs), then he gazes somewhat sadly at a vague point and gently shakes his head. The two cooks look at one another: a certain perplexity hovers in the steamy, smoky room; it is as if, for a second, one felt the wingbeat of the Fates. What now? Tactfully, we look away; after all, we do not want to bear witness to mute confessions of failure or frustration. And so we tiptoe out of the kitchen, musing about the fact that the tensions of our era occasionally encroach on areas in which one would not generally expect them.

After a long wait, curiosity drives us back to the scene of the event. The two cooks sit next to the stove; they are already on a first-name basis (the first cook is named Philip), and they are playing checkers or backgammon—in any case, a board game.

One is delighted, one is relieved of an unpleasant feeling;

nevertheless, it would be utterly wrong to betray by word or deed that this harmony is unusual. On the contrary, one acts as if this were the most natural thing in the world, or at least one of the most natural. One passes by with a greeting, perhaps a jest, lifting the lid of the pot: the gruel looks scarcely any different from the gruels of yore, which were described as "yummy" by our passionately loved, pet-named nannies in between picture-book rhymes and hearty huffing and puffing: granted, no longer as loose and foamy as once, but still: unspoiled. A sample spoonful—and our palates confirm our visual impression. What has good Kuno done? He has increased the amount of cornstarch, whereby he must have been thinking of his bishop, who, as we mentioned initially, lives not only by the laws of God, but also by the —entirely different—rules of calorie-and-protein contents, with which he builds up his monastically meager cells. Who would dare rebuke Kuno? It is entirely our fault that we are aiming at woe and not weal. Our impatient eyes graze the two cooks, who are too good for this era, too mild for this world. Our thoughts wander toward other authorities.

And, not without some wavering, we turn to Gaston. Gaston! Everyone knows him, knows these two all-too-worldly and promising syllables and pronounces them with greater respect than the eloquently lengthy guttural title of some Spanish grandee, and, in any case, with far more palatal, mouth-watering pleasure. It was many years ago that our uncle, stranded in Brussels and residing in its gourmet district, took the irregular member in the line of descendants, us, an adolescent, to the small gourmet restaurant Chez Gas-

ton—where he called the male employees by their first
names, the female by their nicknames, hopeful that this and
similar urbane behavior would arouse the sophisticate in us
with whom he could then rail, in blasphemous complicity, at
what he called the overly straight family oak. Since then,
Gaston, already a man of gastronomic and also physical mag-
nitude, has remained alive and oily in my memory. Despite
the subsequent informative visits to burlesque presentations,
we ourselves never left the ground of bourgeois solidarity—
or at least we returned to it, subdued and purged, after a
secret debauchery; our uncle, however, soon got involved
head over heels in the earrings of a Brazilian adventuress and
he now no longer exists, in the bourgeois sense of the word.
Gaston, however, as was to be expected, is still weaving his
prescribed pattern of life: potent, despotic, and not without
the whims of a man of international consequence and significance, he looms, as massive as a monument to reverence,
from a growing flock of grandchildren, in his parlor, which
is hung with the yellowing, hand-signed photographs of great
mustachioed and bewhiskered statesmen, who, dripping and
tongue-clicking, sporting a napkin under their double chins,
relished Gaston's angouillettes au brisard rôti with gusto and
perhaps contracted a minor, taunting gallbladder complaint.

For Gaston has a thing about oil! It is his element and his
secret, which he nurtures well and wisely, behind his master
apron, on which the traces of decades of beefsteak tartar
stand out in bold, thick splatterings, like a monarch's pen-
manship under a death sentence.

Incidentally, the name *Gaston,* according to the most recent investigations, means *oil* in ancient Wallon. Only—and I must, unfortunately, emphasize this here—this is not the marvelous lemon-scented olive oil, the crop blessed by Apollo and Demeter, the fruit of breezy, silvery-green groves in Argolis and Delphi; rather, it is the viscous Low Flemish oil obtained from the stagnant waters of harshly living, rebellious cities like Bruges and Ghent, and, as reported by several lacemaking Beguines in old chronicles, it even has residues of the earthly remains of the somber counts of Flanders. It is virtually the refuse of the Netherlands. This is simply a small warning for the sensitive gourmet. The reckless gourmand will probably ignore it.

A brief word about Gaston's appearance: a stately, bombastic exterior; people with a heraldic and historical imagination (of whom there are fewer and fewer, alas) might liken him to an aging Northern Romanesque drum major—but only before his meal. After his meal, he looks more like one of the reclining figures in Brueghel's painting of the rich kitchen: a simile, incidentally, in which Gaston himself takes frequent delight; he then feels like one of the great men of his Fatherland, anticipated, virtually sketched by a master who was his peer.

We pick Gaston up at the station. He climbs down from the Ostend/St. Pölten/Niš through-coach (you can transfer to Sofia by way of Cszsewsczs). He carries a wooden suitcase, which his wife carefully tied up with a rope; he wears a brown-and-white checked suit, light gray suede shoes with a fine greasy edge gained in slippery kitchens; he has a sprig of clove in his buttonhole, a sage-drenched silk handkerchief in his breast pocket, rosemary and oil in his hair and mustache, which two props are meticulously parted down the middle, as on a turn-of-the-century sportsman in a painting by the divine Douanier. In the taxi from the station to the kitchen, we outline the situation for him, fully aware that an adjective has no place behind the gastronomical forehead (not to mention a metaphor, which we love so dearly). Gaston nods several times, suitably earnest; after all, this is a consultation, which someone with a calling may be called upon to supply.

The three cooks greet one another, cool but polite. The ice ought to be broken by a jest—preferably one from culinary areas. But that is not everyone's cup of tea. There are no universal rules for such cases, and that is all well and good: if a man has the courage to accept a challenge, he will have the satisfaction of dealing with it in his own way. Herewith, a brief account of the test.

With his fingertips, Gaston pushes up his cuffs and sleeves; with his wrists, he performs a conjuror's flip motion, lifts the lid from the pot, gently grazes the seething surface with the back of his hand, withdraws his hand, studies its back, knits his narrow brow, brings his hand to his cheek, slowly grazes it with the back of his hand, so that tiny lumps of gruel get caught in the stubble of his whiskers; he produces a pocket mirror from his vest, and peers at the reflection of his beard and cheek. Then he shakes his head, takes off his jacket, unbuttons his vest, rolls up his sleeves, and puts on his apron.

We retire. We do not wish to be in the way when he brings out his secret from under his apron. Nor do we know whether he will send out the other cooks so that he need not reveal the perhaps all too simple egg of Columbus of his worldwide renown. In any case, when we enter the kitchen again, they are standing next to him, like eager disciples.

The gruel has grown several shades darker. Gone, alas, gone is the ancient-white, yummy-scrumptious tone; the delicate-skinned surface of the childhood dish is blown away. It has been replaced by a dark oily surface strewn with stamped Caucasian cinnamon like leaves on a puddle in a bleak autumn park. Gaston stirs once and offers us a bit. It tastes strange, to be sure. Unusual. An aroma whose appeal may be slightly reduced by its lack of verifiability. It has a delicate but lasting edge, a small *haut goût* one might almost say, if this concept were not absurd in regard to gruel. But spoiled? No. Not yet.

What now?

Well, precautions have been taken, we have wisely sensed that our Gaston might be able to point out the direction, but not the road leading to the ultimate gruel. We have conducted a protracted and not unencumbered correspondence with the Far East, namely, in the Wong dialect of the southern Chinese provinces, where one finds the vast shipping companies of this truly immense kingdom (and not in the north, as some people erroneously assume). We have been trying to obtain the Chinese sea cook.

He has been waiting for a sign from us. His family name is Lü; his first name, however, is, strangely enough, Marcus, for he was baptized a Christian at a highly active mission station concealed amid waving rice shrubs on the banks of the enormous, muddy yellow Yangtze River. In the course of his checkered life, he has served on any number of ships, from shaky, dainty dinghies to clumsy sailing barks. He has huckstered for any number of gaudy parrots in dockside dives, he has baked any amount of insipid hardtack, dried any amount of dryable meat, salted any number of tiny herrings, and placed sardines so neatly in cans, he has faced any number of one-eyed pirates in Far Eastern territorial waters, and he can tell you a thing or two about sweaty, bare-fisted fighting on bursting ship's boards under ruthless suns—all this with an inscrutably cheery mien, that mirrors his upright soul and childlike humility. His dream about opening a high-class laundry in Cincinnati is about to come true. Wise and single-minded, he has refrained from debauchery and from starting a family, and in this way he has put by many a shiny yen. He intends to be a cook for only a few more years, namely at the rusty range of the merchant frigate *Chung Minh,* a former pleasure yacht, built shortly before the horrors of the Boxer Rebellion, namely for the emperor of China and his blossom-lipped, ivory-fingered consort, the royal couple sailing on it past reedy banks and coral reefs to their famous island gardens, where (it was the unforgettable era of Chinese delights), fanned by slave girls, they took their green tea in grottoes of green jade. This is our new man.

However, to put it tersely: he manages to leave the gruel in a state of dubious edibleness: stone-hard, so that we need a hammer and chisel to detach crystal-shaped fragments, which, to be sure, instantly melt in the mouth like Turkish honey and taste like sweet beef suet—but the gruel is not spoiled. And so, as we must assume, we resort to extreme measures: we must summon the cook of the British chancellor of the exchequer.

But first, a word about the chancellor, a quiet, thoughtful Oxford man, a man for all seasons, who knows how to maintain his equanimity in every situation in life without ever boasting of this knack to others. Deeply rooted in tradition, he knows how to hold his own in a fox hunt, a cricket match, and Parliament; under his narrow upper lip, which has grown stiff in years of self-control, he has his pipes and his sayings, inserting or removing them according to the occasion.

Granted, he is reluctant to lend out his cook, but he has too much self-control to permit any displeasure within himself, much less admit it to himself or even reveal it to others. He did not do any of these things (and only intimate friends in his club recognized his annoyance by his vertical forehead creases) when an order from Queen Victoria forced him to make this sacrifice. Of course, the circumstances were somewhat different than in our case. Because of a minor indisposition, which was accompanied by a broken wheel hub, the venerated monarch could not continue her coach trip through the Western counties and was forced to spend the night in that crooked, wood-creaking, half-timbered Tudor tavern which, in its original 1498 form, is still a mecca for reverential monarchists today, for one of the support beams in the attic came from James I's flagship: an affable donation from the generous queen in gratitude for services beyond the call of duty. Supposedly, however, her gift would have been a bit more generous had the innkeeper been able to serve her a meal. This man, however, one of those bluff, gruff ruffians, a diamond in the rough, with a heart of pure gold—in short, one of those types of whom there are so many (albeit not in real life)—could not have served the monarch anything but a Welsh rarebit, since he, a former sergeant of the Royal Fusiliers, had left one arm on the parade grounds, which loss interfered with his culinary efforts. The queen, whose distaste for cheese has meanwhile become proverbial, was not willing to make do with this food; and so they turned to the chancellor of the exchequer, a promising fifty-year-old MP, whose estate was less than six miles away. His cook came and prepared a Christmas pudding for the queen, which earned him membership in the Order of the Garter as well as an—admittedly noninheritable—title. So much for this event, which struck me as worth mentioning in this context. If the reader does not find my description sufficiently detailed, I recommend that he read Dickens, in whose work this anecdote is not to be found, but who makes up for the omission with merits in other areas.

We know that the chancellor cannot turn down our request without losing something of his already shaky prestige in the eyes of European youth. For over half a century now, he has been talking about international cooperation—indeed, he was the one who coined that lovely phrase. Well, let him put his money where his mouth is.

And the cook comes, in his 1904 carriage, which still runs as if it had been made in 1912. His name is Sir Edward; he wears a high hat, striped trousers, a cutaway, a gray vest, and binoculars around his shoulders. For he has been watching songbirds along the way—his hobby even in rain, snow, hail, or fog: people of his ilk are indifferent to the adversities of weather and time. He enters with a measured tread, greets the other cooks with barely audible—or else all-too-audible— condescension, goes over to the gruel, tastes it, coolly but cordially praises the present state of spoiledness, and says that the Continent is ahead of England in many respects. No one disagrees, for he is right. On the other hand, he says, England has its good points, whereby he is right again. He then removes his hat and binoculars and says that given this grand achievement he can only contribute a mite. A smile of satisfaction at this praise spreads over the faces of the other cooks. Marcus Lü beams, although he does not even know what a mite is. But he always beams, the good man. They move away, tramping nervously and expectantly through the slushy snow in the streets, where lukewarm puffs of wind drive the pedestrians to and fro (for the first signs of spring are in the air); but soon we are lured back to the gruel.

We enter the kitchen. The five cooks are standing around the stove, each with a small spice shaker in his hand, and they are smiling in refreshing international unison and coopera-tion. "After you," Sir Edward is saying to Gaston, who then, with greasy fingers, strews a large pinch of paprika on the gruel, which the Englishman promply covers with a layer of pounded coriander seeds. Old Philip, however, remains loyal to his saffron, while Kuno and Marcus, with grand sweeping gestures, dump in a whole harvest of thyme and pimento, these being instantly devoured by the seething mass, which has once again become fluid. Tables and chairs are covered with bay leaves, nutmeg apples roll across the floor, basil and golden yellow portulaca seem to be sprouting from the niches, not to mention Spanish pepper and salt.

We hop over to the stove. The cooks make room for us. We remove the pot from the flame and peer inside. The seething instantly stops, the mass hardens: a dark-brown crusty clump looks at us with gray crater eyes, under which yellowish lumps of flour and farina sparkle in various colors. We shave a flake off the surface and taste it. The taste is not pleasant, granted. But would a starving man refuse to eat this?

While we ask ourselves this question silently and pensively, the door opens, and a small, fat man enters: dark suit, light gray tie, shiny, spherical head, sweeping out in flesh cascades on one side and in a face on the other. He introduces himself. His name is Blutzbach or Blitzhaus, or something like that. His first name, as he very earnestly claims, is "Howdyoudo."

He produces a tiny vial from his pocket and lets two drops of a violet fluid drip into the porridge. It sizzles, sulfur vapor spreads through the room, and the pot now has a blue clump with yellowish veins, marbled, like Gorgonzola seen in the negative.

One glance is enough: it is done.

The gruel is spoiled.

We cordially thank the cooks, praising their selfless devotion, which, we say, was not in vain. The gruel is garnished with a little fresh parsley and a spicy pickle cut in a fan shape, and is then served hot, in warmed bowls.

SLEEP

for h.m.e.

Let me sleep in the guitar tonight
in the astonished guitar of night
let me rest
       in the broken wood
let my hands sleep
          on its strings
my astonished hands
         let it sleep
the sweet wood
      let my strings
          let the night
rest on the forgotten stops
my broken hands
       let them sleep
on the sweet strings
in the astonished wood

HANS MAGNUS ENZENSBERGER

Tonight, I will sleep in the guitar.

It is lying ready on the rectangular wooden table in my large paneled room with the three high windows. It lies alone, it is not part of an idyllic interior or a Netherlandish still life. I am not planning a painting, I am planning my sleep.

Entering the instrument does not pose any problems, I have checked everything, everything is measured: its soundboard is broken, a crack runs along the wood on either side of the aperture from the outer edge of its curve, petering out halfway between the aperture and the bridge. Thus, the wood is split only along the grain. If the split ran across the grain, the instrument would be useless. The area between the cracks is slightly concave. So this is where I will raise the strings like the wire fence of a prohibited cow pasture, I will slightly push in the picket created by the twofold break, and, pulling myself along the metal strings, I will slide down—cautiously, to keep the cracks from lengthening—and I will then slip through the hole into the body.

I will be aided by the fact that the carved center, which, long before my time, used to make it look like a Gothic church rose, is gone. Time has devoured it, has, incidentally, gnawed on the edges, chewing a bit of ebony and mother-o'-pearl from the intarsia. On the other hand, time has seasoned and darkened the wood, thereby refining the sound.

I will, of course, have to make sure that as I climb in, I assume the physical posture that I wish to have when lying inside, since the resonance space does not permit me to move freely, much less turn over. I will therefore slide in on my back, headfirst (a small act of acrobatic agility that I have already rehearsed a bit); I will then draw along my torso and legs, and thus slip into the rib between the back and the soundboard. Here, I will then manage to make myself at home and lie in such a way that my spine, which I have never seen, but whose upright abilities I have been able to rely on in many a precarious situation, will prove to be a serpent this one and thereby last time, adjusting to the curves of the guitar rib. Once I have found the right position, I will remain in it; I will lie in the wood softly and gently, while inserting my right arm through the aperture and plucking the strings from inside, ad libitum. There is only one chord, my chord. I have tuned the strings to it and it alone. I have forgotten any other fingerings, nor do I need any other, they would only hinder my drowsiness.

That is why my left arm will stay idle. I will place it sideways on my body since the narrow space of the guitar rib will not permit me to keep my arm relaxed at my side. Presumably, I would also be bothered by the hardened beads of glue lining the ridge at irregular intervals. They may not be attractive, but they are the stuff that holds an attractive construction together. Even the noblest instrument utilizes internal imperfections in order to show a perfect face.

I say: the noblest instrument. My guitar is a noble instrument, no doubt, but there are nobler ones. Originally, this bothered me. The vessel of my drowsiness, I thought, should have been a lute, or even its elder sister, the theorbo. These are instruments made of wonderful material, their bellies are pregnant with a gallant past, they bear the breath of the court of Charles IV (the subsequent Louis XI), of bangs and stringy sleeves, under which the musician's deadly stiletto lay as loose as the song in his throat. But these are sentimentalities. What care I in my night about the past of the space in which such a simple action as my sleep occurs! Here I lie, warm and snug, while outside, time rushes by like a gentle but incessant wind (night is the better half of time!), not troubling me with any of the ballast that it blows along. From my place in the wood, every point of eternity, in the past or the future, is equally remote; there should be nothing to make me dizzy.

There is also a practical consideration. One must think practically even in regard to sleep, as in every matter that is ultimately nothing more than a physical function. How am I to lie in the round belly of a lute, the center of gravity shifting with my position? Should I be like a helpless body in the innards of a pitching ship, tumbling to and fro, so that my fingering of the strings from below becomes arbitrary, a matter of chance? No, it is chance and arbitrariness that I wish to escape in sleep! Better to lie wedged between the sides of a less noble instrument and rely on the night, the great equalizer, to equalize this—admittedly minor—distinction in nobility.

I hope for a dark night. Initially, the moon threatens to shine, but it will not reach me. I cannot use it, that lifeless object, which enchants nothing, which, on the contrary, *we* always try to enchant until the futility of such an endeavor finally dawns on us, to our embarrassment. My guitar will lie on the table in such a position that no light will reach it. So that the beams from the three high windows will stream to the floor, atomizing in the glitter of the parquet. And so I will wait for the moon to set: it will do so at eleven twenty-two. Then it will be dark. Granted, even the darkest night has its lighter minutes, areas in which it has become worn and threadbare, with tiny flaws in the thickness of its weave, which already irritated Copernicus. But we can be hopeful that no true obstacle will interfere with the quiet passage of my night. And if ever a strip of lighter darkness should drift by in the passage of the darker darkness, then I shall close my eyes to it. I will not let it upset me.

Am I alone? Yes, I am alone in my guitar, but the room it lies in should not be deserted. A deserted, yet furnished room (albeit containlng only a table, a guitar, and three small window benches) would mean that people have left but might return at any moment. That the rustling of the night could at any moment thicken (unheard of!) into a noise, growing, swelling, and then announcing the return of a tenant. It would mean that there are other people here, absent only momentarily, their absence thus making itself noticeable as a special, intrusive kind of presence, disturbing me, disrupting my sleep. I must populate my night cautiously, animate the room with only a couple of mute witnesses, supernumeraries of the night and custodians of my sleep.

There is also a consideration involving the bodily aspect. My hands are broken; time has them too on its gigantic conscience. I must therefore assume that when sleep touches me, my fingers will no longer be able to perform the one chord that is left for me, so that short of the goal of my arduous preparation, I will get annoyed and angry—a mood hostile to repose, driving away any thought of sleep. Everything would be destroyed, and I would remain in an instrument without music. Here, I have to belay myself. There have to be witnesses, guardians, who, if need be, pluck the strings themselves. Invisible players, men or—far, far, better—women, who echo my music when I am overpowered by sleep, but not yet sleeping, and my hand drops from the strings. I will place those players under the windows, they are to sit on the window benches, with instruments. From there, they will watch over my sleep; but not like Brangaene, combing the night for its dangers; instead they will be self-absorbed, each caught in her own nocturnal world.

I have combed the house for these three figures. I have searched for them systematically. To avoid any charge of negligence, I began in the basement. But there, as I expected, nothing useful was to be found. In the basement, the Fates sit on the cold coals and Fatelike figures with their faces, or if you will, countenances shrouded in black; they are waiting for cheap transportation to a better and more final eternity, although they really do not deserve a better one. A few of them even hum a melody, which I recognized, the Chorus of Prisoners from *Fidelio*. Here are also the mothers, the mothers, before whom a fist rightly recoils, sit there, with crushed handkerchiefs full of precious tears, their sole property, aside from the property that they had to leave and that has therefore grown more precious. I cannot do anything with them, especially the Heroic Ones, who can be recognized by their bony skinniness and their valiant stances. They squat in a circle, around a laurel wreath that was never laid on the Tomb of the Unknown Soldier. It is made of Lübeck marzipan (which these mothers must never find out), but it has petrified utterly, the ribbons are ragged and ripped by spiders, of which there are countless ones here, chiefly daddy longlegs. And what else? Off to the side, over a children's table, sits an aging high-school teacher; he is working on a multivolumed history of the future. His beard has grown through the table. No, there was really nothing to be found here!

I could leave out the ground floor. It consists of nothing but the rectangular room with three windows, where I plan to sleep. The room is prepared, cleared out, dusted, the floor is waxed, the brass polished, nothing can hide in the niches or cracks.

I next went upstairs. The elaborate wooden banister had once been white; today it is ivory-colored, and it creaks in a certain place. Right there where my then young, today still soldierly and youthful, sister felt a sudden death wish and leaped down to the first floor, thus overcoming her death wish. Today, she is the mother of four children.

In the upper rooms, there are heirloom timepieces, that is all. Here, I have always managed to maintain beneficent emptiness, so that I need not start when I open a door and enter a room. The emptiness is not the terrifying emptiness of a house that is about to be taken possession of and furnished; it is the emptiness of a house that has already been lived in and furnished. It has mellowed, it has discarded the horror of Gemütlichkeit, and it may now look forward to the calmer remainder of the future. In the last room, however, there is a wooden chest with copper fittings. Inside, wrapped in airy tulle with laces and veils, lie the earthly remains of a prematurely deceased aunt, my mother's youngest sister. Little more is left of her than a smile, which death struck when it whooshed past. She has been spared a lot, people said back then, whereby they probably meant not only the rib resection (my aunt, like so many darling people back then, was consumptive and was about to be operated on), but also the general anxious future, now the past. For the earlier one dies, the more things one is spared; that is the simple equation of popular wisdom, which thus attributes great happiness to the numerous, albeit increasingly fewer unborn. Be that as it may, there is no one here whom I can use as a witness of my sleep.

So I open the pantry door and, with vanishing hope, I ascend the attic stairs to the flotsam that the waves of time wash under the roof. At every step, the air grows heavier and warmer. A warmth that has been stored up in many summers and has never dissipated.

There are many things here. Half on the stairway stands a pilot as if he had only just been carried up here and had not yet found the right place. His face is in a helmet with several layers of glass, between which small fish swim, excreting oxygen. Next to him stands a knight's suit of armor, which has always stood here, and behind which I have always expected a forebear who ambushed merchants in Kocher Valley, robbing them, castrating them himself, and selling them as eunuchs to Oriental courts. But today I know that nothing so estimable is concealed behind the armor; it is a venerable minister of state in a vest that turned gray a long time ago, with a pince-nez and a stand-up collar, a Maltese cross and a rosary around his neck, the stamp of diligence on his forehead and a medal for the courage of his convictions on his lapel, awarded by the Office of Public Decorations—a servant of many servants of many systems before he wound up here, upstanding rather than resting in peace. A bit farther on in the room, in a light beam filled with dancing dust, I see the wheeled cast-iron sewing machine. The Thursday seamstress sits there; she became a hunchback while still alive, because of long, unrequited love; but she is always filled with cheerful ditties; stiff, galvanized into a statue of renunciation, she has become one with the cast of the frame, beyond all sleep, deader than dead, a monument.

None of this is very encouraging. I can see that I will have to go deeper. Nevertheless, I continue. A cello leans against a diagonal support as if deposited there temporarily, with the player soon to return. For a split second, I wonder whether I should sleep in *this* instrument. It is roomier, seems more conducive to sleep (how often has it made me sleepy in a concert!), its curvature looks so restful, it describes an adagio. But I must think ahead; to think of sleep means to think far ahead, and so I reject the cello. Granted, the rib is nice and wide, my spine would wish to imitate its curvature, but our bodies would part company at my buttocks. For at the point at which the waist of the instrument narrows down to the bridge, two double ribs curve inward, and if I bend my knees and wrap them over the rib, my lower thighs will loom upward helplessly. This would be uncomfortable. And who is to play the instrument? I cannot reach through the narrow F hole and wield a bow, and if someone else held the bow, I would be

143

the twofold victim of the player and the piece. A pianissimo would prickle, and a forte would be a roaring inferno. Besides, I now see that someone else is already sleeping inside. It is Pablo Casals, the once famous cellist. His breath already rattles slightly, but it is calm; however, his heart, his most valuable part, is working as always. A wreath of oxeye daisies lies gently on the bald head of the valiant Catalan, may he rest in peace—he has earned the right to do so.

Right behind the cello, leaning against the wall, sits Albert Schweitzer. His pith helmet has slid way down into his face, but is kept from falling by the mustache, in which the remains of his jungle meal are nestling. He is asleep, and he seems to be where grumpy old age and drunkenness reveal the same symptoms in sleep.

I morosely decide not to seek here any further. I must evidently find my three nocturnal handmaidens in other regions. I must step out of space, into time, and go back in time by outstripping it.

In time, I have managed to catch up with my three watchwomen. The choice was not easy, for I had to weigh all qualities, everything from the soul, to the body, to the fingertips, especially the latter: the seismographic dials of the soul and, simultaneously, the indiscreet and mobile ramifications of the body, which, in my case, must also know how to play a few forgotten chords on the strings.

The first is Mona Lisa. At first sight, she seemed to meet an unexpected number of conditions. But at second, deeper, and more prudent sight, she appeared to meet no condition whatsoever. It was only at third sight, which should always penetrate the object, that I realized she satisfied my demand. I was hindered not so much by the vision of the great Leonardo as the dirty-greenish condition of his painting, which is unfavorable to the sitter. Granted there is something peculiar about the sitter herself. I do not mind the fact that she has no eyebrows and smiles only with the left half of her mouth. She was a lady, and in her day only fishwives had eyebrows, and only courtesans smiled with both halves of their mouths. More serious, however, is the expression of a fleeting but always present idiocy lurking behind this face. Today it is known that La Gioconda actually went through periods of imbecility. This gave her, in the eyes of other people, the aura of mystery whose spell the well-meaning admirer of this likeness still thinks he feels today. I myself am little touched by this mystery, but I see no blemish in its roots. I owe it to myself and my sleep to place a Florentine on one of my three window benches, and who is more Florentine than Mona Lisa? She has a noble posture; furthermore, she commands silence, and that is what I need. Her hands are soft as though the child's knuckles had been thoroughly kneaded, but she can play a few chords on the lute, I know it. A young painter taught them to her when she was still Lisa Gherardini, and she would have liked him to teach her more, but he felt nothing for the opposite sex. Later on, after getting rid of a rival for the pope's favor, he became a cardinal; but that is a different story. Mona Lisa also knows a few songs. Her old nurse from Urbino, who had also been her mother's nurse, sang these songs to the baby, and the adult, for the most part, starts anxiously singing them whenever her spouse, a cattle dealer smelling of hides and leather, tries to approach her tenderly. These are simple songs, songs whose sounds drift gently through the suites of rooms; they are heard across the river and through the streets. It is the most lulling thing in the world. Listen to someone singing many streets away, plucking a stringed instrument, and you already feel the wish to do nothing but sleep. And that is why I need La Gioconda, transposed into the image of my night in my guitar.

I could get the second watchwoman from real life, and I did not hesitate to do so. For she is Sister Antonia. The reader does not know her, will never know her, and I will try not to make him too painfully aware of this lack. All she has in common with Mona Lisa is an Italian background and the corresponding sound of her name. Suor Antonia. She utterly lacks nobility, an ivory quality; she is all matter, a heavy mass, while Mona Lisa is a slender apparition. Sister Antonia knows nothing of Mona Lisa, she probably never even heard of Leonardo Da Vinci, and the word *Renaissance* would presumably be synonymous for her with *Resurrection,* and only the Resurrection of the Lord, her Lord—not mine, I have no Lord. I know her well. She tended me when I was ill, and by giving her a role here as an equal partner of two great ladies from time, I am thanking her for her loving care, although it is by no means pure gratitude that led me to this choice. In the course of my life, I have been well treated by many people whom I would never make guardians of my sleep.

Suor Antonia is fat and very broad—how fat and broad cannot be determined under the many yards of rough, black serge and starched white linen, the ample habit of the Vincentian. The shape of her head is likewise a deep secret, behind the multitudinous sail of the veil and the coif, which forces her to look straight ahead. She does not exist naked, the very word *body* is, if applied to her, blasphemous. She knows little aside from her tiny birthplace, Surava, and the not much larger town where the hospital is located. There, she knows her mother superior, her sisters in the order, and her father confessor (what could she possibly confess?), the rosary under the fold of her robes, the inventory of the hospital, and her patients, who remain sick for her even if they recover, and who become truly healthy only when they have died. Indeed, she feels a tactfully restrained pity for all who have made themselves comfortable in this world. She herself, though sound in body and thus belonging to this world, knows that her soul is already at home in the next world. There, she will discard all the trumpery she wears here, especially her thick, black woolen stockings, which she must darn in her spare time, like a penitent. When she was young, this work struck her as the essence of all worldly idleness, but the tempest in her has long since abated, and now she manages to cover any all-too-worldly things with prayer.

Her face is brown, her hands are red and coarse, they know how to handle bedpans and hot-water bottles, but never the guitar of my night. Hence, she will not be able to help out if my broken hands fail or drop back in sleep. The two other watchwomen will have to pitch in. She will then sit at her window, and gaze amiably and unswervingly at her two sisters in sleep-watching, thinking of God and darning her black woolen stockings, which she has to bring along so as not to be idle. She must not fall asleep, not she. Nor will she want to. I need her to stay awake when I lie here in my guitar, I need her the way a scared pale boy needs his black mammy, who, if called upon in time, can see to it that he will never again be afraid of the dark. It is not that I am afraid of the dark; no, I have long since overcome the child in the man. Nor is this child a vestige of childhood, no indeed, he grows with my increasing age and the concomitantly increasing fear of the span of time remaining for the man and the fear of what may come after this span. I have no fear of any spans, for I will enter my guitar. And while I may not believe that anything else will come, I do wish to have Antonia nearby, for she does not need to believe it because she knows it, knows it with all her soul. This is her great role in the process of my sleep.

However, Lisa and Antonia are not enough. All three windows must be occupied. Furthermore, the slight element that the first two have in common, the southern element, must be balanced by something else, something alien to it, to prevent any false bliss due to moods. I do not wish to revel, I wish to sleep. And that is why, after initial wavering, but then with increasing conviction, I have decided on Mary Stuart.

My choice is the middle Mary Stuart. I have selected her from the three months between Lord Darnley, her second husband, the murderer of her secretary Rizzio, and Lord Bothwell, her third husband, the murderer of her second husband. Evening is setting in, her day's work is done: she has written twenty-eight letters, seven to Queen Elizabeth, thereby weaving a bit of her legend. Dreaming about realizing her passion and her fruitless ambition (qualities that seldom permit her to smile), she sits with her theorbo in my room, on the window bench, which, in this case, has become a chair at the window of her intimate wood-paneled study in Holyrood Castle or else in Dunbar Castle or Stirling Castle; but no matter what the castle, she sits under a velvet tapestry, under an embroidered, gold-brocaded coat of arms, next to a fireplace in whose chinks the scab of darkest history has collected and will keep on collecting. She gazes out across endless Scottish pine forests, which do not reveal in which of the three castles she is sitting.

What does she dream? In any case, these are dreams that are alien to Sister Antonia, that a Mona Lisa might emulate were she familiar with the preconditions. Mary Stuart may be dreaming of Bothwell, whom she loves, but not so deeply that she would not kill him once she no longer loved him. Between dreams, she fingers a chord, let us say A-B-D-C sharp, and her thoughts ramble on: Who will be his murderer? A future husband? G-F sharp-C-G. It would have to be done in utter secrecy: poison would be best. But that is just what those Protestants are waiting for! G sharp-A-B-F. Well, there's time, things have not reached that pass yet, for now she cannot live without him. G-F sharp . . .

There she sits, with her chords and cogitations, which she learned as a child at the French royal court, and which will help my sleep, for these chords and cogitations have been atoned for: it is not for nothing that I was forced to reach so far back in time. She sits, in a millstone collar, sleeve puffs, wasp waist, in a marlotte of velvet and brocade, on her bosom a gold cross which she often sucks mentally, an embroidered coif on her dark hair, which, to her lasting, paralyzing dismay, is starting to get thin, increasingly thin, until one day (but she does not know this yet, and she knows it no longer when she attends my sleep) her wig falls into the dust and her bald head rolls from the scaffold to the ground, gaped at in embarrassed silence by the headsmen with doffed toques and loudly barked at by her lap dog, which hops out of the back of the headless body in which it sank its teeth during the execution. But this too is no longer my concern. If one took Sister Antonia uncovered (as God created her albeit not as He let her grow), she too would be bald. In contrast, Mona Lisa has soft, smooth hair, *morbido.* . . .

Thus, it is these three figures who sit in the windows tonight. From these three bodies I have built the spirit that is to dominate my room. Peacefully, I lie in the bosom of this spirit, to which I have entrusted myself in seeking sleep. And even if idiocy and murder are interwoven in it, nevertheless it does not exhale the repulsive breath of those murderers and idiots whose presence impels me to find the long sleep in my guitar. I lie in the sweet wood of the guitar, in the dark space, in the body, in good, healthy dryness, in the night, relaxed, stretched out, my body emulating curves, like a huge horizontal *S*, my buttocks lowest as if, drawn by the center of the earth, I were sinking backward to that center, devoted to my own chord, which I have fingered and to which I have tuned the strings. And when I can no longer finger it, when my hand sinks down the outside, then two of my three guardians will take up the interplay as a prelude until I sleep and beyond, while the third guardian, diverted by nothing but her God, who is not mine, will watch over my sleep, waking beyond it, and darning, always darning.

Here I lie, plucking my chord, pausing for a fermata, listening to the silken rustle of Mona Lisa, the starched crackling of Mary Stuart; I do not hear Sister Antonia, she is darning. The house is still; outside, the night murmurs. Upstairs, the clocks have stopped. I do not need them, for what happens here does not happen in time. Time? What would the morning be like after such a night? Shall I lift the strings and climb out of the aperture, rub my eyes and look around the bright room, like someone who has landed on the moon and realizes that it resembles the earth? Shall I let the strings rebound while I climb out in order to face a day that will wipe out my precious conjectures as though I had not painstakingly constructed a night?

No. Here I lie, here I stay. Here I shall pluck my chord until my hand sinks down on the wood outside, and then . . .

I shall listen—almost but not quite asleep—to the chords of the guardians, the lady with the slightly feeble-minded smile, her pointed fingertips resting on the wood between chords; I listen to the cracking of her wrists when the royal murderess takes hold of the fingerboard, fine skin lies on fine wood. I listen to an antiphony that never resounds, an unsung, barely remembered, only vaguely imagined song that sings itself. It sings itself in the remoteness of the Florentine lady and in the remoteness of the Scottish queen, and from the transverse wall I hear the silence of the Vincentian nun darning God's sock.

Once again, in a drowsily abrupt attempt, my hand sweeps over the strings, then glides down the outer wall of the instrument, over its broken wood and, dangling to and fro just once more, it remains hanging at the wrist. The chords of the players grow softer, the fermatas longer, the melody lingers faintly in the space between us. Almost asleep. I play along as my dream begins; I play their chords mentally since I have now forgotten my chord, the night is lying on it. My guardians have reached for metal strings and may still be reaching for them, but no longer making them quiver; and I hear their fingers, one hesitating finger after another, gradually settle, tapping gently, then only tentatively, on the guitar body, on the thin soundboard under which I lie, my ear to the wood. . . .

I hear the fingertips adhering to the wood, then, barely on the wood, grazing the surface, gliding downward, between the strings and the wood, then between the wood and the night, and then suspended forever in the night. . . .

while Antonia keeps watch and eternally darns wool.

I lie inside; outside, someone watches and darns, two others sleep two different sleeps. . . .

and inside, I sink into my own slumber and I sleep. . . .

under the sweet strings

in the astonished wood.

MISSIVES
TO MAX

Once again, as you, dear Max, have probably ascertained, another year has passed, and I do not know if you feel as I do: but I am getting a wee bit tired of this everlasting cycle, to which various factors contribute—factors whose author I would not care to name in this connection, lest I, who am peaceful by nature, incur difficulties whose inconceivable consequences I would be forced to endure.

In any case, I am excellently shielded against the new year, I am insured against burglary, fire, hail, and life, not to mention an act of God, about which I seldom speak, that is, only when such an act makes itself noticeable, and even then not always, indeed, not at all at that point. The dog has had its day, the sheep are separated from the goats, the chicken is in the pot, the pot has its lid, I've feathered my nest, thrown in the sponge, under a rising snow cover, leaving it to the tobogganists (if you will forgive the word) to cut their coat according to its cloth.

Of course, where shall I now take the flowers, and where the sunshine, and where the shade of the earth?—I do not know. The last is certainly not the least—it is something that would require an enormous effort even in the summer, for, as everyone knows, shade utterly resists being captured and transplanted; otherwise, I would be surrounded by shade and shadows. If I really need flowers, which is highly unlikely, then I naturally get them from the greenhouse; and as for the sunshine—forget it, or rather, I *could* forget it if someone else got it, which is not the case. I have never gotten any to forget.

The summer was not exactly big, but big enough, I am not complaining. After all, a summer ought not to be *too* big, but I know: it cannot be big enough for some people. The apple did not fall far from the tree trunk, which made for a far easier harvest. But someone let the winds blow on the fields, which I took as inconsiderate if not offensive; at the very least, it showed bad manners—not to mention a bad background, which is too painful to mention. Someone also commanded the final fruits to be full, and gave them another two southern days, which were unbearable, but at least they bore enough to fill the cellar. But someone (I do not know whether it was the same person) also drove the final sweetness into the heavy wine. I did not catch the fellow, he probably drove by night. And now, for better or worse, I must prepare for a sweet, heavy vintage—but never mind: the vintages are not getting any lighter; on the other hand, the ages are getting less and less sweet. Have you noticed? Can you recall even a single sweet age?

Still and all, I have built a house. It is not yet dry. The walls are still somewhat speechless and cold, while outside the triple-pane windows, the snow is falling on monosyllabic things, like the field and the mead, the path and the grove, the bush and the shrub, the brook and the pond, and so forth. as well as on bisyllabic things, like hedgerows and spruces, poplars and meadows, clearings and forests. All this, as you may have gleaned from this list, boils down to environment, which, incidentally, I duly protect, so long as it leaves me be, which, alas, is not always the case.

Be that as it may: before the new year with its unpleasant and pleasant surprises (the latter are rare if not obsolescent) takes its course, tears will have to be dried, theories confirmed, and hairs split. For soon, the first snow will come, and with it the first loipes. They usually come from Wanne-Eickel or, as the educated call it, Castrop-Rauxel. They are heterozesque, and unfortunately also noisy and social, and they breed by way of pushiness. They get on nerves, from which they can be easily shooed away by short notices. Except that from there, they usually get into the underwear (which I never overwear), and from there, at unguarded moments (one cannot guard every moment), they usually get under your skin, from where one cannot easily dislodge them, for that is where they breed. I find this ill-bred, but then I simply give it short shrift, evaluate it as a symptom, and place it *ad acta,* where many a symptom lies or rather is consigned to oblivion.

I would advise you, dear Max, to do the same (I mean the act of *ad acta* putting, not the consignment to oblivion), in case you are not already doing it and in case I did not receive this advice from you. I have become so forgetful, thank goodness.

I forget birthdays, red-letter days, national holidays, name days, my collar size, chest size, waist size, shoe size, and blood group, of which, so far as I know, there are only three, aside from one that occurs seldom, and has probably been already bought up by collectors. Sometimes, I also forget my limits (5′8″, 160 lb), but at such times I can ask my neighbor, so long as he is available. However, he prefers to be elsewhere in precisely such cases of doubt, dilemma, or forgetfulness; and since *one* of these three possibilities is *always* the case, I have never laid eyes on this neighbor. But that may be partly because he knows very well how I would love him, namely as myself, and since that is not very much, he is probably seeking someone else, whose neighbor he wishes to be, someone who loves himself more than I love myself, and who can therefore love him appropriately as his neighbor, that is, as himself, or he may even be seeking someone who loves him more than himself, a difficult quest to be sure, and I would let him know as much if ever I laid eyes on him. On the other hand, I do not want to hinder him from seeking someone else, since I would thereby get a different neighbor, who might be less demanding of my brotherly love, which, of course, does not necessarily mean that he would be available in case of doubt, dilemma, or forgetfulness.

·   ·   ·

It occurs to me that I have a problem. I do not know how it came to me; it must have developed gradually, or else someone dumped it on me while I slept—I know little about the background, genesis, or makeup of problems; in any case, it happened a long time ago. Be that as it may: my problem has grown rather large, indeed, over-life-sized (as if life were not already large enough and its size still had to be coped with even when it was over!). It is, as you can imagine, a *genuine* problem: I would never put up with less. It is a rather complicated problem, and my friends, or at least the well-meaning among them, advise me to solve it. But I cannot make up my mind to do so, I have gotten used to it. Sometimes, I wonder: what would I be without my problem? And of course I am unable to respond. I would certainly not be the same, whereby I am not saying that I insist on always being the same. If you are interested in my problem, dear Max, which, however, I consider highly unlikely, I would be glad to lend it to you. Or do you have one of your own? In that case, I naturally do not care to place an additional burden on you, for I know how strenuous and enervating and time-wasting such a proper problem can be. Moreover, I believe, although I may be wrong, that problems are as untransferable as identity cards, identity crises, or hermetic texts, or pregnancies—or complexes, neuroses, psychoses, or scabies, whereby I am not quite certain whether the last is a mental disorder, a skin disease, or a bug, in which last case it *could* be transmitted, but that, of course, makes no difference in this case. I am certain you catch my drift.

Naturally, I also have a neurosis. Not a compulsive, but a

voluntary one. It is relatively easy to cultivate, almost easier than a rose, because it is less dependent on the weather and unconnected to the seasons. A single wish trauma can serve as its point of departure. Repress it, and soon everything proceeds on its own. Your libido awakens, bright-eyed and bushy-tailed, and refers to a referential person, who instantly rolls it onto your superego (how super is your ego?) without your suffering the slightest loss of an object. You only have to begin to sublimate your hostility in time—which I would advise you to do anyway—so that the id can eavesdrop on everything as if it were behind a sound barrier (preferable to an unsound barrier). But then, I advise you, give in to it properly. For such an opportunity seldom knocks twice in life —to be sure, if at all, then only in life.

It is better to give than to receive, according to the Gospel according to Luke. But, frankly, I find the opposite to be true, although naturally it depends on how one construes the word *better.* If it means that one feels better, then I can only say for myself that I would feel better if I received a million rather than gave it, which would also probably plunge me into greater debt, so that I would be forced to take out a long-term mortgage, which, at an interest rate of ten percent, supported by short-term loans, would not be very favorable (since at the rate of fifteen percent, it would climb to nine hundred ninety-nine points on the Dow Jones Index), so that it would have to be guaranteed by gilt-edged mortgage bonds. But perhaps this calculation contains an error—I am not a *real* expert in this field. *Entre nous:* I do not even know how one takes out a bond, much less a gilt-edged one. But please do not tell anyone, it would be bad for my reputation. For me, a checking account is sort of like a check-in count, and as for a Czech count—I dare not even speculate what that might be—it sounds like a medieval torture instrument. All I know is that credit is better than debit. In case you did not know that, then please note it and act accordingly, that is, receive rather than give. In any event, you ought to take professional advice to heart, if you know how to take something to heart.

However, if the word *better* has an ethical meaning, then I can only express my amazement at the crass immorality of this statement. For by giving, I make the person to whom I give a receiver, thus depriving him of his moral betterment, at least in the area of ownership and thereby liquidity, of course (I cannot say whether he can make the loss good in other ways—I do not know him well enough for that); thus, I am behaving very egotistically in order to purchase my betterment, unless I could be sure that the receiver would be ready to interpret the statement ethically and instantly pass the gift on to someone else, in order to make someone, whose strict principles he is familiar with, a receiver—needless to say, without profiting or profiteering from the gift, so that he may partake of ethical betterment. But this new receiver, in turn, values his ethical betterment and transfers the sum to the account of a third person, who, Christian as he is, passes it on to a fourth, who, however, is not willing to forgo his betterment, and therefore passes the sum, considerably increased by interest—for better or worse—to the account of a fifth person, and so forth, until someone, who does not give a damn about salvation, prefers to keep the money and then squanders it or, if you will, dissipates it on his dissolute life-style. So if a person cares about his betterment (and there are more such people than is generally assumed!), he should quickly throw the gift away, like yesterday's newspaper, or pour it into the sea, like coffee in Brazil. But there is nothing about that in the Gospels; indeed, there was no such thing as coffee back then.

In any case, it is better to travel light, without bales or ballast, without a load on your body or your mind, or a monkey on your back or your head in a noose or in the clouds, and especially without mincing matters, for mincing them, as people usually find out much too late, is harmful, which is why one should consult a doctor at the very first symptom.

I would like to have become someone else, wouldn't you? But we should have started earlier; now, it is too late. Indeed, it would not be so bad never to have been born in the first place, but that happens more and more seldom, I could scarcely list any cases, except right off the bat; but you certainly would not care for that, and you are right not to, I do not like that either. We have been given our lives—I do find that expression highly euphemistic, but be that as it may: gifts from parents or from people who *become* parents only by the act of giving can be neither rejected nor passed on, for one would never find the right taker. Besides, at the time of the giving, one does not yet possess the right vocabulary to make the thing palatable to others. Oh well, it would not be possible to return the gift anyway. But I am amazed that the recipient's screams of protest right after the act of giving do not give the givers food for thought. Perhaps they already *have* food for thought, but do not realize it since they are rather inexperienced in this area. Still, we, as recipients of the gift, have no opportunity anyway to exploit this food for thought, we would not even know where to begin. And so, for better or worse, we begin with life, as if nothing had happened.

In English, being in danger of life is the same as being in danger of your death, which all boils down to a matter of life and death. Now that gives one food for thought. For it means that, for example, the danger of forming a habit is the same as the danger of breaking a habit, and the danger of collapse is the same as the danger of noncollapse. Now something does not make sense here. Unfortunately, that danger of collapse does not exist for architectural monstrosities, while the danger of life can, strictly speaking, be escaped only by a still-birth.

For years now, I have been taking psychopharmacological drugs, which, as everyone knows, change one's personality, and I have been looking forward to becoming unrecognizable. But people recognize me instantly, even when I do not recognize *them;* perhaps they are taking more powerful psychopharmacological drugs. And perhaps their personalities have therefore changed so greatly that those people recognize *me* as someone completely different, which I, of course, would be if my psychopharmacological drugs were as powerful as theirs, so that I am, so to speak, recognized on a different level, unless the similar makeup of the drugs has made the levels identical again, so that I would be standing alone again, so to speak, with my inadequate psychopharmacological drugs. Yet something speaks against that: namely, the fact that even people who do *not* take psychopharmacological drugs recognize me instantly and unfailingly, thereby demonstrating de facto the difference of levels, unless I am misinterpreting this behavior because of an overdose of psychopharmacological drugs. I also do not know whether other takers of psychopharmacological drugs recognize each other as quickly as they used to, *before* they were taking them; that is, perhaps they *too* mistake one another for others, and who knows, perhaps they *are* others; but *I,* despite my psychopharmacological drugs, have remained objectively the same, while others, including those who do *not* take psychopharmacological drugs, would have changed, so that psychopharmacological drugs would again make them the same as they were.

Ultimately, everything boils down to the question: Who am I? This sufficiently well-known question of identity, which, psychopharmacological drugs or not, one instantly recognizes as such, insofar as one can still recognize something that is coming out of one's ears, especially if one is taking psychopharmacological drugs. At this point, some people reach for *Who's Who?* which actually confuses me. Just who is *really* who anyway? Do *you* know? Then please tell me, preferably in a letter. Some people have gotten lost while seeking their identities; but unfortunately, most of them return after finding themselves and henceforth give up psychopharmacological drugs. The identity that such a person has found is usually not his; rather, it belongs to someone who has voluntarily cast it off; but the person who has found it does not realize it is not his, otherwise he would have a relapse. These feel fine everywhere and no matter what, especially in their shoes.

Well, be that as it may: I would like to have become someone else, for instance, someone who kicks against the pricks, except that I do not know what pricks are, nor do I know anyone who could tell me, much less does it, unless he is a closet prick-kicker.

Perhaps I should have become a voice crying in the wilderness, but that struck me as all too theatrical and behind the times. Granted, if no one were listening, I would be alone with my theatricality, perhaps simply *too* alone. Besides, this activity leaves one hoarse. Many of these vocalists have lost their voice and have been forced to choose a different vocation.

I wish I had become a diameter, for instance, a profession I find so broadening, it would have widened my horizon, kept me on the straight and narrow, but also made me well-rounded. However, when I was young (I majored in casuistics, as you know, and minored in viniculture, and now I am, so to speak, a major casuist and a minor viniculturalist), those areas were still in their swaddling clothes, which are no longer what they used to be, and babies have to bear the brunt. But, of course, babies too are no longer what they used to be. Take me, for example: I am now sixty-five, and if and when you read this, you will be seventy-one or even seventy-two, and I would be almost sixty-seven, whether you read it or not. Since I know that you are a slow reader, we may both be even older. You see, I too am anything but a fast reader, much less a fast brooder. On the contrary, I frequently spend days brooding over a single sentence, and often what I hatch is not worth mentioning. But then worth-mentioning is a horse of another color, not a pleasant color; that is, it all depends on what you do with it, in which case it is really not so different from other horses.

As a minor viniculturalist, I have often been urged, usually by well-meaning people, to do something worthwhile in a pinch. But I am not sure that this would be suitable for me. You see, I do not feel that pinching is ever really worth any while; I suspect that it actually whiles away its worth. I can picture a traveling salesman, sitting over (really behind) his beer and reaching under the skirt of a barmaid. Now just whose while is that worth? Champagne, of course, is something else again (and what isn't?), it is a beverage that shields against both sham *and* pain, stress and strain, wind and waves—especially the latter—as you brave the storm and storm the braves. But I am no longer up to such downs. Perhaps I am viewing the matter too romantically—I view many things too romantically. Then again, there are many things that I do not view romantically enough.

When I was a child, I wanted to be a rear admiral, since, as I was told, rearing is so important. *Rear* is a lovely word; it sounds like *rare* or *real:* rare realities and real rarities. Real rear admirals are rare: like Admiral Horthy, who was reared for the front, although he was rarely accused of being a front for the rear guard. But then, he rarely guarded his flanks.

Incidentally, I am impressed by dropouts. After retiring from a retiring life as a shepherd or flower gardener or fruit grower, they enter heavy industry, maximizing their energy potential and working their way up the corporate ladder to top positions in the steel-processing branch, which demands total commitment, absolutely and relentlessly. After all, for a long time, I mistook coronary thrombosis for something else: not so much a flower as a Late Baroque wind instrument resembling a fanfare; why, I even thought I had once heard a concerto for coronary thrombosis and orchestra in F sharp minor. And you can imagine how its fans are faring. But then I discovered that it actually refers to the formation or presence of a blood clot in a blood vessel of the heart—with not a trace of music. However, my alarm, provoked by this misunderstanding, has long since wound down, and now it is lying at my feet, and it has grown fond of me, I have gotten used to living with it.

I would also have loved to become a professor of tautology at the University of Walla Walla. But many far more qualified people are scrambling for that chair. Ultimately, I am nothing but a tautophile dilettante. One should have no illusions about one's own abilities, although there are different opinions on the matter, opinions to be taken seriously—although I cannot cite any offhand.

Or I could have been a market researcher with my own institute and two assistants. My research would go back to the ultimate sources, the markets of the Assyrian period, about which much too little is known. Then to the agora of Athens in the Age of Pericles and then on to the medieval church fairs with Maypoles, sausage booths, and pardoners, while fiddles, cornets, and krummhorns accompanied the people doing their St. Vitus' dance, and the drunks, cripples, and lepers rolled along the walls of stone and planks, spooning their millet gruel, and bellowing and babbling as they gambled away their fat alms—it must have been an earsplitting din, you probably could not hear yourself think, but people did not think that much back then, and certainly not by hearsay. Besides, I do not think it matters one way or another whether you can hear yourself think, so long as the person you speak to thinks he understands you. But I know that many other people think differently about this matter, which does not help matters much, since they will never be able to hear themselves think.

Then on to the Vanity Fairs, where people sell themselves short and sell out, that being the long and short of it. Then up to and down to the carnivals of our childhood, with peppermint canes, tunnels of horrors, teddy bears, unshelled almonds, wax museums, and bearded ladies. Although they can no longer be researched—I mean the carnivals, not the bearded ladies, but I guess it holds for them too; one would probably have more luck with the wax museums and their variant, the torture chambers. It was all so long ago, dear Max, don't you agree? And anything that was not long ago gets older from one day to the next, faster than things long forgotten. Yesterday's hormone household is today's family planning and tomorrow's ecological problem—if tomorrow ever comes. For instance, who today still remembers Bobby Vinton or Brigitte Bardot or Fischer or Dieskau, not to mention the shah's Soraya or the astronauts, who, as we all know, can be mass-produced today by pressure-casting in polyester —highly gifted high-school students have already come up with a model of the Milky Way probe and have been duly lauded by the Universal Science Council and been awarded a two-week stay in Disneyland or in the Canary Islands. Something that was merely an ulterior motive yesterday is ripe for the picking today and will simply be used to wrap garbage tomorrow. I therefore advise you to do as I do. Purchase a few yards of it right away, preferably Sanforized and stainless, which the garbageman has to guarantee with a ninety-day warranty. Make sure it is not too hot. And you can also use it as a hedge against inflation, which will probably trim your hedge now that topiary art is in and gardens are out. Try selling short if you want to take a long view—so long as your hedge is not so short that it does not cast a shadow on coming events. In this way, you will never be caught short especially if you put your bushel in the shade. Above all, do not darken any door, and remember that there is a light at the end of the tunnel. Incidentally, in case there is danger of an earthquake, a risk that keeps growing until it is finally so overshadowed by the earthquake itself that people no longer think of the risk, you ought to get a Richter scale, which, I gather, can be bought at a reasonable price. Make sure it is open-ended on the top. In general, I would caution you against things that are open-ended on the bottom.

Whenever I hear the term "open forms," which is seldom heard in my mountain village, I instantly recall the ribbed, parti-colored tin molds with which children bake sand pies on the beach—or *would* bake if there were still any beaches. Sometimes, I also recall our dear departed friend and the brickworks of his childhood: they were located in Lebus (stressed on the second syllable and declined according to the fourth declension, *not* the second declension, that is, not Lebus, lebi, etc., but Lebus, leboris, etc.) on the Mississippi, or rather between the Mississipi and the Mistersippi, but not, as some people maintain, between the Ms.sippi and the Missippi, known for its Renaissance, of special delight to regional researchers. After all, the Ms.sippi has become a profession, created by Betty Friedan, the first to practice it with some measure of success. Not a strenuous profession, more of a trade than a trade-off, and not to be traded in. Well, as someone once (perhaps even more than once, perhaps even several times) said: You cannot have *everything*. But that is a different story. Indeed, there are quite a number of stories, don't you think?

But, back to our dear departed friend! Do you remember? He never knew whether he should pay the piper and dance to his tune or be paid *by* the piper for dancing to his tune. In the end, he did neither. May he rest in peace—or in pieces as the case may be.

I, on the other hand, have reached a conclusion after burning my bridges behind me and not being led up the garden path, which is somewhat perilous now because of the melting snow. Others may have a horizon, but I have mountains, to which one grows accustomed, you only have to meet them halfway, especially at the beginning. Eventually, they come and meet *you* halfway, especially in a blizzard—the only thing you can do then is close your eyes—that is, it helps you to cope with the mountains meeting you halfway, not with the blizzard. On the other hand, the good is at hand, within reach, so that sometimes, if I feel like it, I rejoice without frightening my neighbors, of which I have only one, to be sure, or rather *had*, or more precisely: a *female* neighbor, a little old lady with snow-white hair—you know *how* white snow can be, and you might eventually explain it to me, there is no hurry—it would be an ideal place for a conversation. I mean a real conversation, I never indulge in small talk. But I usually have no one to converse with. So I talk to myself. Since I speak Middle High German without an accent, sometimes even being mistaken for a Middle High German (a misunderstanding that I could usually clear up if I *wanted* to clear it up, which was not always the case), I usually talk to myself in Middle High German without fear of being recorded or overheard, much less answered. In the winter, I can hear the snow goose honk and the hoary fox bark and vice versa. Frankly, they sound awful, but they are the only animals that can still articulate clear umlauts, which, of course, are now useless, but that is not their fault, they do their best. In mating season, they even emit an occasional diphthong, which, however, occurs so seldom and so irregularly as to carry little ornithological weight. But, as I see, this is easily dealt with, especially, of course, if one has never felt truly at home in the area of ornithology, which is the case with me. How about you?

In the spring, I can hear the grass grow. Sometimes, it

sounds a bit shrill, but then again so tempting that I could just eat it up, which temptation I have always managed to resist. Yes, dear Max, God knows I have always admired the great blue yonder, but never let it get too close for comfort, which, as you know, is something I am not in the habit of getting. I may say about myself that I have actually found it.

So, things are going well for me. I wake up with a song on my lips, which, to be sure, gets somewhat boring since it is always the same song: "Old MacDonald Had a Farm," a subject that is relatively irrelevant to my conscious life, much as I love animals. I wonder whether it could be the fault of my lips, which are a bit dry at times; to deal with this problem, I purchased some lip balm, the label of which says that this "salve has been buffered in the acid realm." I do not know whether this is a positive or a negative statement; it probably depends on *how* acid the realm is and how far it extends. For a while, a different song was on my lips: "Jingle Bells." But by the time I came to the words "all the way," which, incidentally, I consider weak, I stopped, for I had focused entirely on waking up, the program of which does not include any concern for long distances. Nor does our era have any room for such a concern. I have also given up focusing; nothing much comes of it.

Early in the morning, after the song, especially if I feel like it, when mild masses of Atlantic air are permeating our climatic sector (or rather dousing it), a possible low-pressure system over the Azores is still far from our continent, so that there is some likelihood of precipitation later this afternoon.

I like listening to the grass grow. I make my way through stems and stalks cautiously, to avoid befouling any nest, for grass is not only full of widows, it is also and especially full of birds—mostly quail, loons, gray plovers, mockingbirds, and bass fiddles; the latter, as one might possibly assume, does not refer to some category of operatic singing, it is the name for a type of pseudocormorant. Once, using my binoculars, I spotted a spotted fever, it looked like a pigeon, which it is (without quite realizing it). It occurs rarely and only symptomatically, just as Asian flu occurs only in Asia and the French disease only in France.

Then I arrive at the lake, which is quiet, peaceful, sometimes radiant, and even inviting. I resist this invitation, I can resist anything but temptation. How about you? The water runs deep, as I can gather from its stillness, and, I might almost assert (if not firmly and emphatically), that there is something sacred and sober about it. In any case, it is so sober that these swans, which are sometimes completely intoxicated from kisses (I do not know the kissers, nor have I ever encountered them here—perhaps they too kiss only at night), become sober again, perhaps sacredly sober; but I am not quite sure for I am not very conversant with the sacred. I do not fish, the water is not dark enough; I believe that the sacred is never dark, but, of course, I may be mistaken.

On the way home, I sometimes try to see the forest, but am unable to do so because of all the trees. They always seem to be getting in the way, and I have heard similar complaints from other people who have come to see the forest. In fact, one can scarcely see the trees because of all the leaves and branches. I try to talk to the trees, but they do not listen to me. Perhaps because I speak to them in Middle High German. And if medievalists do come by, then only once in a blue moon, and even then not regularly. In any case, I have never encountered a living soul here—much less a dead one. If at all, then it was a *living* soul. Of course, one does not often encounter any soul that has been released from its body. The opposite is more often the case, albeit not the rule.

It is as silent here as in the wood of myth, or roughly so. All one hears, occasionally, is a bird, whose loud, gurgling twitter moved the delegates to, and participants of, the Congress for Problems of Humanity, Humaneness, and Sentiment (1904, Pittsburgh, Ohio) to resolve with an overwhelming majority in its concluding vote that beauty is for such birds. The opponents of this resolution (a diminutive minority, that carried no weight, much less the vote) become possessed, each in turn, and remained possessed down to the third and fourth generation.

Sometimes, at night, a dog barks on some lonely farm by the edge of the forest. I then tell myself that a barking dog never bites. But this comfortable old saying does not put my mind at ease. For I know it and you know it, but the question is: Does the dog know it? We really have no handle on what a dog knows. The fact that he is man's best friend would actually testify to the meagerness of his intellectual faculties, if we were certain that the dog's best friend is man, which has not been demonstrated. Strictly speaking, the statement about biting and barking would also mean that a biting dog never barks. Ergo, dogs would have to be subdivided not only into two hundred forty-two breeds (I always come up with only two hundred forty because I forget about the Illinois Greyhound and the Lower Saxon Cur), but also into dogs that bark and dogs that bite. Perhaps that is why some people have two dogs, one for barking and one for biting, which, however, is useless in that either the barker drives away an intruder before the biter has a chance to bite, or the biter bites first, anticipating the barker and thereby depriving him of his livelihood. Perhaps, however, the biting and the barking take place simultaneously, for the barking dog does not have to come as close to the victim as the biting dog—or else either does both, which is possible; after all, there are people who talk with their mouths full. Indeed, perhaps there are also dogs that neither bark nor bite; but then one wonders: What good are they? Naturally, we also have to consider hunting. But that would be broaching a subject that does not really interest me; I sincerely hope you do not mind, for I believe that this subject does not fall within your purview either. In any case, the potential victim is a pessimist (optimistic victims are few and far between, and entirely lacking here), and he therefore leans toward the likelihood that, as I have already considered, a single dog has taken over both functions, first barking at the victim and then biting him, or vice versa, of course—although, so far as the victim is concerned, it no longer matters which comes first, the barking or the biting. Of course, so far as the dog's owner is concerned, this is a horse of a different color; the owner's aim is to tighten his belt and save on the high overhead of maintaining a second dog, for it is by no means true that the biting dog bites off a piece of the bitten victim. That is, the biter's primary goal in biting is not nutrition, although the latter would, no doubt, be more desirable for the dog's owner, since dog food is highly vulnerable to inflation. Dog biscuits always cost twice what they did the previous year, as I was recently assured (without my even asking, of course) by the owner of two dreadful, but faithful Illyrian bloodhounds.

Granted, it would be wonderful if this highly ambivalent proverb could be taken literally, so that, at the sound of the dog barking out there at the edge of the forest, I would think: If I were now taking a solitary stroll through this delightful night air, this barking dog would not bite me. On the other hand, I would not know whether some second dog, wrapped in profound silence, was impatiently waiting next to him, gasping bloodthirstily as it prepared to bite. Furthermore, I would take such a solitary stroll only in order to enjoy the nocturnal peace and quiet and to delight in its soothing effect, which would be destroyed by the barking dog. But if the night were truly full of peace and quiet, no barking anywhere, and suddenly a silent dog emerged from the darkness and bit me, I would certainly not be very satisfied. Sometimes I really do not know whether *I* am being difficult or whether everyone else is being difficult; only I am the most easygoing person in the world, or let us say, *one* of the most easygoing (or is it easiest-going?): I never lay claim to being unique, although perhaps I should.

174

.   .   .

Otherwise, however, my position is firm, resolute, and ada-
mant, not to mention unshakable. An airy place over soft
meadows and cogent grounds, high and sublime. (I have not
yet gotten to feel that it is only a step from the sublime to the
ridiculous.)

From here, I recently saw the *Ding an sich,* the thing per
se. It lay in a thicket of blueberries, raspberries, beriberies,
and danburies, as though laid by a gigantic bird, in an encir-
cled nest, where no one would find it, certainly not a thinker.
On the one hand, it was round, on the other, oval (you are
well aware of that eternal on-the-one hand/on-the-other-
hand), and it was about the size of a medicine ball, as I picture
it (I do not know how *you* picture a medicine ball, of course).
It was greenish gray, unprepossessing, as well as indescrib-
able—in any case, nothing to carry on about. Nevertheless,
someone must have carried it, unless it was gone with the
wind or wafted by the breeze—but it struck me as too weighty
for that. Perhaps it dissolved; I think to myself, perhaps one
or more Kantians passed by, knowing that the thing per se
eludes carrying and stops being as a result of the attempt at
postpossessing it. That was probably why they wanted to
consider it only from afar, not knowing that it resists consideration—which I could have told them. In any case, we are
once again dealing with one of those enigmas that always
arise when the result of a system of thought goes astray in
reality, where it has no business being in the first place (or
the last, for that matter). For, in order to remain a concept,
the thing per se (unlike us human beings, incidentally), must

elude any possession (pre or post). Quod erat demonstrandum.

Well, every so often, people come by—to be sure, more Hegelians than Kantians, in any case mostly contemporaries, if not my fellowmen; then, too, some people visit me in order to determine what we have in common, which succeeds as good as never. Then, in order to avoid misunderstandings, I fall back on my Middle High German, thereby leaving my visitor speechless, which he already is, although he does not know it—how many people think the opposite is true! In general, I live a sheltered life; I am a man of few words, and now and then I read a good palimpsest or the proposition of Anaximander or a dangling preposition, or I play the ocarina —a tune or fortune about love and death, sometimes about rise and fall. Recently, I even went to the Fortune Society. I instantly realized that our society has to be changed; I changed it and went home early. Ever since, I have not had much interest in societies.

Incidentally, the Grim Reaper galloped by in late summer. We were about to begin the aftermath, the buttercups, potato tops, and sour creams were still in full blossom, the breeze was wafting through the aspen leaves, the meadows were more floral than flowery, common swifts and not-so-common ones, screeching awfully (though hardly full of awe), soared every evening over my position and other positions, the lettuce was about to shoot—when that Grim Reaper came riding up. His teeth chattering, but not very chatty, he sat slightly hunched (he's no spring chicken, something he shares with us), in the saddle of his old gray mare. We hadn't seen one another for a long time—in fact, we had never even met before, but facts need not apply, and I know why! And I shouted, perhaps a bit too exuberantly—for he rode past, he was not after me, after all, he was after a little old lady, who, after a hard life of sorrow and suffering, supposedly cried out in the face of death: "That's all I needed!" *I* shouted to him: "Death, where is thy sting?" "Kicked off with my pricks!" he shouted back, perhaps a bit too confident of victory for my taste, which you know, for he knows, of course, that I may have the last word, but he has the Last Things, so to speak —and then that fellow actually shouted at me: "Nature, where is thy bosom!" As though I had asked him to play a guessing game with me. "Why nature?" I shouted, and all at once I was overcome by a quota of quotations, which seldom happens, but this was the Goethe Year. I added, "Nature and spirit, that is not how one speaks to Christians!" "What do you mean 'Christians'?" he shouted back, and there he had me. I had not known that he knew full well. I fell silent, if I remember correctly, subdued, to be sure, but sheepish. I felt misunderstood, as I often do. Perhaps I am too sensitive, too vulnerable, and too ill-humored, although I have always considered myself easy to humor—sometimes, usually toward evening, I actually feel that I am a loser. But be that as it may. Loss is what helps us find ourselves.

"Hell, where is thy victory?!" Instead of lapsing into a subdued silence, *that* is what I should have shouted at the Grim Reaper; that would have silenced him, if not given him food for thought. But it did not occur to me. I am slow on the uptake, and also fallible, ultimately a bit asocial and aloof, but gifted.

I picture hell to be like the Ziller Valley. Or like the tulip fields of Holland, or the passion plays at Oberammergau. Or like St.-Moritz in the summer. Every other day, a nine-hour passion play. In between, a day of music with a view of tulips. Every evening, a concert by the Vienna Choir Boys or the Regensburg Cathedral sparrows, in case they are not the same boys or sparrows. In the morning, the Moldau, conducted by Karajan, or something on original instruments, handmade and untuned by Harnoncourt. Or trio sonatas by Telemann, Piccolini, Ricotta, dal'Abaco, Locatelli, or by Telemann, Rosenmüller, Eppenbauer, Father and Son, Wenzlsberger, Telemann, Muffat, Telemann, or by Hans Christian Bach or by Wilhelm August Bach or by Carl Maria Bach or by Johann Wolfgang Bach or Wilhelm Friedemann Bach or by Georg Telemann Bach for nine recorders and continuo. Performed by Giselher Schramm, Hiroshima Kajumi, Rainer Weckerle, Kazuzo Kozikawe, Irmengard Wäwerich Sträubler, Mitsubishi Toyota, Hedwig Wunderlich-Buhbe, Kazakumi Kozikawe—presumably the brother or sister or wife or husband of Kakuzo Kozikawe, perhaps even the father or the son—Osakazu Okakura, and Karameli Tzubishi, with Luitgard-Maria Tashayumi-Spechtle on the continuo (incidentally, a not unimportant continuist, who, I fear, is still to be heard from).

In view of nature (in Holland, in the form of a billion tulips; in St.-Moritz, in the form of a mountain world, and both lovely and majestic at once, or rather grandiose, that is, in its most agreeable and most popular variant), I sit (forgive the dreadful picture) over my campari soda, counting the incipient skin cancers of my fellowmen and trying to estimate their life expectancies, for all of them sit there, expecting life, overcome over and over again by its delightful thrill, albeit not for long. Thus I lie in the sun on my chaise longue, and next to me sits a fellowman or even someone close to me and tells me his dreams, one after the other, for hours, pitilessly. Now and then, he forgets a detail and starts all over again. And when he has told me all his dreams, he is replaced by someone else, who tells me all the plots of all the novels he has read during the past few years, starting with *Dr. Zhivago*, to the three hundred twenty-two novels of Simenon, whose real name, as we all know, is Simon and who comes from Katowice, just as Proust's real name, as we all know, was Pressburger and he came from Budwiče. Thomas Mann, as we all know, etc. . . . And then he insolently claims that I ought to read all those novels, and he promises me "great reading pleasure." How little we human beings really know one another, I then think—and not *only* then, of course.

Or else the person sitting next to me is someone whose age, however advanced it may be, you cannot tell; and he tells me how things used to be, when a chicken cost only fifty cents and three eggs four cents or four eggs three cents, and a gross of eggs no more than a cord of wood and vice versa. The summers when the grand hotels of Engadin were full of Russian princes, owners of a thousand versts and ten thousand souls or vice versa, and they drunkenly rolled across the Persian carpets, sipping champagne from the slippers of their

favorite ballerinas and shooting one another when they discovered that two of them had shared a favorite ballerina.
When the American billionaires were still shoeshine boys or
newsboys, when live elephants or real Wesendonck-bred
horses still lumbered across the stage in *Aida* or *Die Walküre*
respectively. When the entire theater broke into sobs over
Pavlova's dying swan, Caruso's pagliaccio got under your
skin, Paul Wegener's Mephistopheles gave you goose bumps,
and children didn't have to go to school on the kaiser's
birthday.

Or else someone sits next to me and tries to persuade me
that the beta enyzymes or endymes or ethymes contained in
vegetable proteins, especially in Solonaceae, and above all in
sorrel, or in animal protein, deprive the body of natural
lecithin, causing serious encephalosis with cirrhotic side
effects, and usually a terminal case of nephrosclerosis. Head-
aches, stitches in the side, and vomiting indicate that the
spleen has been incurably undermined, and that the gallbladder has also been impaired, especially if one drinks. (I drink.)
One shot of Fernet-Branca, even if thinned down with heavy
hydrogen, can paralyze the entire intestinal peristalsis, for it
contains enough tannic acid to tan forty pigeon's eggs the size
of pigeon-egg-sized hailstones; this is due to its large amount
of formic acid, which, taken orally, is far more harmful than
hexamethylenetetramine, which, after all, can be found in all
dairy products today, especially in rose-covered cottage
cheese. A single foxglove, as the two Nobel laureates Fitz-
gerald and Blumenbeim have demonstrated, has a completely
lethal effect on reptiles, salamanders, amphibians, and certain

fissipeds. Much better to go to heaven, but they have yogurt there. Soon, there will be nowhere left to go to.

Yes, I drink. You too? I think I see the glass in your hand, but that may be an optical illusion; they *are* frequent, especially when one drinks. On the other hand, I have stopped smoking, and ever since I stopped, I no longer cough, but that is no real substitute. Still, I cannot complain, much as I would like to. I feel fine. Ever since we were told to conserve energy, I have stopped walking, I drive everywhere now. Sometimes, albeit not too often, I wonder what we will do with the extra energy. But the answer is, of course: conserve. Every child knows that. Soon, only children will know it.

Under these circumstances, I obviously do not climb stairs anymore, I only use elevators. Naturally, this can induce a feeling of frustration in a different way. In the hotel Österreichischer Hof in Salzburg, a sign in the elevator says: "Only for six people." You can imagine that on a quiet morning during nonfestival seasons, one sometimes has to wait a long time until there are six people. It is especially annoying, of course, when the sixth person shows up with his or her spouse, and, since I am alone, my (incidentally, innate) good manners dictate that I allow the couple to enter first, so that I again stand there alone, waiting for a new crew, whereby the same constellation might result again, in which case I naturally do not repeat the good-manners maneuver, leaving it up to a different lone person to be the victim. But he is already inside the elevator, staring at the floor. I therefore concentrate on yesterday's menu, which is tacked up inside the elevator. Nevertheless, I do have a bad conscience now and then, for I think of the lady who arrives in her room, only to realize that her husband, who is waiting below, has the key, and she does not know when she will see her husband again, since he (assuming he is as well-mannered as I) has to give way to a couple downstairs; however, she must know best whether he is given to such sacrifices. Naturally, while pursuing these thoughts, I forget that not every person has my basic consistency, husbanding his energy as I do mine, whereby he might choose the steps, albeit glared at by someone hurrying over, a person who might have been the sixth, unless some other couple has hurried up, and *he too* must take the stairs.

By the way, I am painting again. My works are sometimes objective, sometimes nonobjective, and sometimes so unobjectionable that there is nothing to be seen on the canvas, which always puts my mind profoundly at ease. One of my pigment tubes says that it contains genuine artist's pigments. Quite a number of artists must have believed that. Altogether, I find that the implementation of life is becoming crueler and crueler. The geometrically increasing love of the environment, to which I am naturally succumbing little by little, is producing a certain misanthropy, to which I am likewise succumbing little by little. This is evinced above all in my consumption of food. I have stopped eating farmer's liverwurst if only because I have to think of the poor widow, assuming the ground-up farmer was married. Recently, in a grocery store, I saw a family meat pie. In such a thoroughgoing use, there is at least no survivor left to mourn the others. Nevertheless, I cannot make up my mind to consume this product; there are families and there are families, and I do not know to which of the two categories the one processed here belongs. Granted, as I am informed, the customer has the right to a complete list of ingredients, but I nevertheless miss the indication of the degree of quality, especially since the product is offered in an economy size. Economy sizes always depress me anyway, nearly as much as plastic bathroom cups, colored bed linen, or humor magazines.

When it comes to food, I am sensitive. You can offer me the yummiest French toast or the most opulent Sicilian pizza —and wild horses would not drag me to a devil's food cake. I find hush puppies and the lion's share repulsive, I am never so hungry that I could eat a horse, and everything human is alien to me. Thus, recently, on a hotel menu, I saw a brown Betty. I would rather hold my peace about that, if you do not mind; I can think of *too many* things to say. Incidentally, I also never eat any chicken I have not known personally, and any catnip can go nip a cat, as far as I am concerned.

Recently, in a haberdashery, I saw a sign that said, TROU-SERS, GREATLY REDUCED. I reflected that here, at least, in a lapidary manner, someone was focusing on the reduction of the human being, especially the male, no mincing of matters, no point to the crown of creation. A bar of soap I bought recently was labeled: "The deodorant of the future." I am not quite certain what was meant. Will this soap deodorize the future or will this soap deodorize us ourselves, so that we can face the future fresh and odorless, capable of overcoming its perhaps not exclusively agreeable scents or whiffs or fumes?

.   .   .

183

According to the newspapers, butchers in a southern town have finally succeeded in creating an 800-foot-long frankfurter, most likely after a number of frustrations, for one must pay a high prices for such innovations, which are usually bought with human lives—just think of the pyramids. A few of these pioneers may not even have lived to see the end of the frankfurter, they may be lying buried under it, if not . . . no, not that. Thus, as you can see, dear Max, progress everywhere. Before it becomes ubiquitous (and there are certain indications that it will reach us at any moment), you ought to come here. Who knows what it will be like afterward. Presumably, the same everywhere, which also has its good side in that we will no longer have any wanderlust; on the other hand, staying around might not be all that tempting either. In any case, travel involves certain dangers—and not only travel.

Incidentally, I read in yesterday's paper that a gradual change is being planned in the rail system (wherever it is making tracks). This strikes me as a relative item of news, insofar as it does not involve a partial dismissal of the railroad staff or even an occasional reduction of the rail network or a temporary interruption.

Change for change. This is not, as the scientists are trying (with considerable success) to make us think, the eleventh, much less the twenty-fifth hour; hence, there is no reason to panic, since (as I need not tell you), it is already two forty-five, and any panic would be an exercise in futility. Any executive can tell you that, albeit for very different reasons. Granted, science may be swiftly outstripping us, but the scientists are lagging far behind, trying to catch up with it—in vain, naturally. I see them running, over sticks and stones, shouting, gesticulating, with butterfly nets and specimen boxes, as if they were born yesterday, which they were not, of course—they were born the day before yesterday.

My house will soon be dry. The walls will no longer stand speechless, they will recover the use of their speech faculties, launching into Middle High German. Scarcely a man is still alive who understands it, but most people have trouble enough with modern languages. Since my flags have no wings, I cannot get them to fly. I will have to wait until our national holiday. The walls are already growing ears, but otherwise they are empty. As yet, there is no handwriting on the walls; besides, how much would it say anyhow? A portrait of my problem would be nice, but it won't hold still long enough, it always keeps looking for my sore point. No use my trying to explain to it that I am a mere mortal, all over, except perhaps in my soul; yet it tries to avoid my soul, and its efforts are equally useless, of course.

Be that as it may, my place is getting cozier all the time, none of my screws are loose, the bats are gone from my belfrey, and everything is out of the closet (except for whatever is in it). I have liked closets ever since I was knee-high to a grasshopper; they have always had a relevance and a priority for me: nine on a scale of one to ten. I am waiting in vain for the Year of the Closet. Every room will have a bucket with a drop in it, designed by Beuys, and the spaces between the cracks will be done by Walter de Maria, he is already hard at work. A word or two are still hovering in the air, but, wanting a response, they will probably vanish into thin air, from whence they most likely came. And what looks like a garbage dump will radiate with the verdant intensity of ribwort, sorrel, and luxuriant weeds—especially hemlock. There is a bucket hanging over the well, and that is where the broken pitchers must be lying.

So you can depend on a good drop. I drink it out of a hollowed stone, in which, to be sure, it sometimes oozes out, so that even a sampling tube will not help. I then reach for the bottle. The wine here is neither fruity nor hearty, neither full-bodied nor full-minded; it is drinkable. But do not expect any champagne punch. For the champagne that *I* have here is good only for launching ships, and that is the only use I make of it.

I will regale you well, the kitchen fathers will make sure of that. For simplicity's sake, I have left the kitchen in the village, for, as you have probably heard, it is the one and only redeeming one, and I would not want to have my fellowmen forfeit this opportunity, especially those who would rather give than receive, of whom there are probably not all too many.

Apropos kitchen fathers: as you probably know, too many cooks spoil the broth. *How* many has never been determined statistically. At present, that is, extremely late, world gastronomy (also known as International Cuisine, which probably means as much to you as it does to me) is taking steps to do a correct count. But I am worried that not *all* cooks are participating in spoiling the broth or undermining the basis of broth-making by means of a boycott of all manufacturers of ingredients. For I feel that expecting a real cook to prepare this highly unhealthy dish for children (I believe it will be placed on the list of carcinogenic foods next year) is like expecting a ship's captain to row me across the garden pond. Broth should be the responsibility of the wet nurse, who, while stirring, utterly intimidates her little victim with an insidious lullaby; or the governess, who, in case of noneating, will threaten to call the child eater, who is already supposedly standing behind the basement door; or the nanny, who warns that nothing must be spilled, otherwise she will be forced to notify the boogeyman; or other vanished figures of our golden childhood. That is why the determination of many cooks to spoil the broth strikes me as an all-too-understandable act of defiance, nay, I might almost call it a necessary reaction, and I do call it that, and will do so with anyone who wishes to hear it—naturally, few people wish to hear it, especially compared with those who hear *at all.* I am so deeply impressed by the solidarity of this still unknown number of refuseniks that I look askance at any cook who does *not* spoil the broth, assuming I encounter him and instantly recognize him as a broth spoiler. I have trained my eyes toward this goal. And my eyes should then say: You conformist you: you help to prepare the broth that we have to eat with a long spoon. Naturally, I do not know whether my eyes really do say that; eyes are often misunderstood, as you know. That puts them on a par with words, intentions, and modes of behavior, which is par for the course, of course.

.　　　.　　　.

After midnight, I am visited by the short-order cook, whom I have saved from my childhood. During the day, he takes care of my vitamin needs, and it is his nightly task to roll salami slices, wrap cold canned asparagus in ham rolls, slice onions into thin wheels, stick olives on salt sticks, plane cheese into slicettes, open pickles into fans, octagonize tomatoes, trim radishes into teeth, dice up the gelatin and distribute the dim-yellow cubes across the plate, bed cold cuts on wilted lettuce, adorn the edge of the plate with potato chips and parsley, and serve the completed structure with supermarket pumpernickel and pats of butter in tinfoil. You see, he comes from the Midwest, and he is indeed very short, and as cold as his cuts, especially his shoulder, which he can show anyone who longs to see it, and if it falls short of one's longing, and you need more meat for your drink, he can also roast or grill a loin. You will have to gift-wrap your presents for him. Perhaps you will pass an appropriate boutique.

I will not visit you in New York, for I do not fly. I will not enter any means of transportation that cannot back up or stop short in the element in which it moves forward. But if ever you come to Zurich again, I will visit you and, if you like, pay the visit myself, for you might find the joie de vivre of this city rather expensive. The polyglottery of the main thoroughfare, where almost every passerby speaks a second language, which he never fully masters, has thoroughly taken me in, so allow me to take you out. I am especially charmed by those costly watches in the shop windows, timepieces whose lapis lazuli faces have neither numbers nor strokes. They never give you the time of day, so that one never knows whose hour has struck, and you can piece time together only approximately, the result being that you can no more tell time than the watches can, though, frankly, I would never dream of telling time *anything.* Just you wait: soon, watches with hands (or even fingers) will be thrown on the market or lie on purple velvet; such watches have a twenty-four-karat quartz, which one can never see or hear, but only have a dim inkling of. All ticking is gone, everything is still, but something is moving inside, something that does not reveal itself as yet. What can it be? In any case, man (please forgive the rhetoric, which always overcomes me when I speak about man or the like)— man will finally realize the true value of five o'clock shadow, but by then it will be too late.

We can also go on a manhunt. I would like to shoot a few nice specimens. Incidentally, it is unfortunate that other big cities are not dealing with the problem of overpopulation in such a sportly manner. A certain Tyrolean spa (I would not care to mention its name since it is Ehrwald) has a hotel shooting every summer. However, I do not know whether the hotel guests shoot at the natives or at each other, or the natives at the hotel guests or at each other. The latter strikes me as unlikely, since it might offend the public. I do not know very much about tourism (although I know what I like), but as I see it, if a spa keeps digging graves for a growing number of guests, it will soon dig its own grave and stew in its own juice. On the other hand, it will have a short season around All

Saints' Day and All Souls' Day, for then the survivors come to put flowers on the graves. However, the victims' bodies are probably transplanted to their hometowns, for such a tiny village can probably ill afford an efficient and reliable funeral parlor. I can imagine that the undertaker and coffin maker are laughing up their sleeves—but who does not do so every now and again! Incidentally, the law provides for specific seasons: duck season, turkey season, and so forth. But how do the ducks and turkeys know when their season is scheduled to come around? After all, most hotels *lower* their prices during the off-season.

Naturally, such procedures are unnecessary out here, in the country. Oldsters and youngsters get along famously, in peace and quiet, and when the situation permits or even demands it, they achieve silent grandeur. And if their equilibrium is ever off balance, then someone may be helped into the beyond, which is actually in back of the back of beyond. It is a better world, but where is there a worse world? And if ours is a worse world, could it ever become better, and if so, would it be better than the better world? So whatever people do, they will do away with people, throwing the baby out with the bath, while a great deal of water flows over the dam—a circumstance that has already benefited certain people over the centuries.

Thus, you can see: an equilibrium prevails here. Each person's new broom sweeps clean, and the people all vie to sweep everything under the rug, because, not living in glass houses, they can throw all the stones they like. A lot of stones are thrown about, causing no end and no beginning of confusion, while the rugs keep rising higher and higher, and the stones keep getting thrown about. With so many stones passing back and forth, each person is, to some extent, both a giver and a receiver, so that we may welcome the fact that betterment is not the issue here.

On the other hand, everyone here knows that you can deal with a situation and even cope with it by wasting no words, much less mincing matters. This has a great advantage: everything is or seems to be in order, which boils down to the same thing. No tourist has ever stumbled over a wasted word or minced matter; each person retains the few words he calls his own, especially the ones that *are* his own; and he certainly does not give up the borrowed ones; rather, he guards them like the apple of his eye or more.

Thus, a number of outsiders have been frustrated here, and a number of writers have struggled in vain to find the expression of interhuman communication, since he has been denied the appropriate interhuman experience, and, with his tail between his legs (I mean this figuratively, of course, or should I say: *not* figuratively?), he has returned to the city, empty-handed, having learned (or unlearned) his lesson.

I, on the other hand, am still here: here I am and here I shall stay, and, if I put aside the barking dog (which I would love to do, but there is no side-putting here), I live in peace and quiet. To be sure, I have the power saws, the ringing and tolling, the mooing and crowing, the bleating and carpet beating to contend with. But I like to contend, if it is not all too time-consuming, especially mornings. So here I sit, working on the opus of my old age, entitled *The Closet in Myth, Legend, and History.* Incidentally, as I have been told gratis, it fills a real need, for who today is still working on a metaphysics of everyday life? This question is rhetorical; that is why I am not striving for an answer, unless you yourself are working on such a topic.

Granted, I too had once set my sights on a higher goal, namely a biography of Anaximander, but this did not work out, for I did not know whether he made his proposition as a young man or as a venerable sage, or whether he also made a second proposition. There is a great deal of evidence to support this assumption.

In any case, I live alone with my old short-order cook and my neurosis. The two of them get along famously, one feeds the other, although I only feel it (I mean the neurosis) when there is a change in air pressure. And naturally, I also live with my problem, which, however, has become my pet, eating from my hand, even when I only give it my little finger, in which case it bites the hand that feeds it.

I am quite safe from identity crises. I am—as I hope I have sufficiently demonstrated—always changing, both hopeless and hopeful, lightened and enlightened, inverted and introverted, disgruntled and yet trying to regain my grunt. In short, if I my fill my mouth, I am a polyhistorian of myself and my environment, which all too readily goes off on tangents, losing sight of itself, so long as we keep our eyes peeled and our wits about us.

On the other hand, every individual is free to bring along his own identity crisis. I am willing, to some extent, to help guests find themselves. However, the search is usually as useless as any search for something with which you have had it up to here and which is coming out of your ears, which is not the only reactive phenomenon, which some less sympathetic person would not go along with, which I fully understood. When the heart is full, the tongue will speak, so we can be happy that the stomach does not join in. Nevertheless, some people have occasionally gotten caught in the act, thereby freeing themselves. But you, dear Max, are, so far as I know, free, and you should therefore come before the stroke of three. All problems, neuroses, and psychoses will fly out the window. Everything will go, dear Max, our ears, our eyes, but if we laugh last, we will laugh best.

Subject/Object

Many scholars have focused on the illogical connections of words in locutions with a transposed subject and object; they have attributed this phenomenon to such factors as "mental laziness," "inadequate mental acuteness," and "unclear conceptualizations."

Stöcklein, whose small but substantial paper "Bedeutungswandel der Wörter" (The Semantic Transformation of Words) discusses verbal confusions and similar phenomena, seems to point chiefly at an inadequate analysis of the realities involved. On page 70, he writes: "The characteristic of convenience or the law of indolence or inertia seems to be close to the lack of strict logical discrimination: in language, phenomena that are mutually distinct are nevertheless designated in the same manner because the conception of each one is the same. The speaker himself can note that the conception is unclear and the expression imprecise; his main concern, however, is to express something, in order to arouse a specific conception in the hearer. The expression may be incorrect, so long as it is understood, primarily only in the given context." Stöcklein is not thinking of a semantic transposition. He lists some expressions that can be called incorrect in terms of logic: "Der Krug läuft aus, rinnt," analogous to the expression "das Wasser läuft, rinnt aus dem Krug"; similar to Latin *cruor manat* and *culter manat cruore;* "die Räume fliessen von Blut" alongside "das Blut fliesst in den Räumen," and so forth. In regard to these expressions, Stöcklein comments: "There is no change of meaning here since the notion attached to the verbs is the same in each context." Björn Carlberg, *Subjektvertauschung and Objectvertauschung im Deutschen* (1948), p. 34.

Behaghel attributes the new, semasiologically unjustified verbal connections to an inadequacy in the faculties of perception and thinking. His list of verbs with fixed and movable objects ends with the remark: "These shifts reveal the very frequent weakness of language in regard to the casual linking of things." This same view appears elsewhere in his *Syntax,* which he points out to the reader. In § 104, an explanation is offered for the *enallage adjectivi:* "This shift derives from a certain weakness in perception and thinking." In § 614, the following is stated about verbs with multiple meanings: "This phenomenon actually springs from a frequent weakness in grasping a causal connection, so that not only a stone is cast but also a puppy [German *werfen* means both "throw" and "whelp." Trans.]; not only water runs into a pitcher, but a pitcher runs full of water, the wall teems with flies, and so forth. Also see the discussion of the adjective in § 147. Regarding verbs of motion, there is the additional factor that the person who sets something in motion will also start moving himself. If you hit someone else, then your arm will also hit, i.e., move [German *schlagen* means "hit" but also "move." Trans.]. If you are chasing a deer, then you are moving swiftly [German *jagen* means "hunt," but also "dash." Trans.], and a car jolts around because it is jolted back and forth."

In general, however, we must bear in mind that the speaker is conscious of the true state of affairs even when the linquistic expression for it does not deviate too greatly from the earlier usage. Krüger emphasizes this: "It is not unimportant to realize that the conception of the thing has not really been discarded." It may be obfuscated, and we "require some amount of reflection to realize that we . . . are not really thinking what our language seems to be saying."

(ibid., p. 35)

p. 154
HOLDERLIN
Half of Life

Hang the land into the lake
With yellow pears
And full of wild roses,
You gracious swans,
and drunk with kisses
You dip your heads
Into the sacredly sober water.

Woe me, where shall I find
The flowers in winter, and where
The sunshine,
And the shade of the earth?

The walls stand
Speechless and cold, the flags
Flutter in the wind.

p. 154
RAINER MARIA RILKE
Autumn Day

Lord: it is time. The summer was so big.
Now place your shadow on the sundial faces,
and let the winds blow on the fields and meadows.

Command the final fruits to fullness now;
give them another pair of southern days,
urge them on to completion and then drive
the final sweetness into the heavy wine.

The man without a house will build no house.
The man who is alone will stay alone,
will keep awake, and read, and write long letters,
and restlessly go wandering up and down
the paths of gardens while the leaves are drifting.

pp. 177 ff.
The First Epistle of Paul the Apostle to the
Corinthians, 15:54–55

Death is swallowed up in victory. O death, where is thy
sting? O grave, where is thy victory?

pp. 158 ff.
The Gospel according to Luke

p. 171
Fisherboy (singing in the boat):
The lake is smiling, it looks so inviting.
The boy fell asleep on the verdant shore.

FRIEDRICH VON SCHILLER: *Wilhelm Tell*

p. 171
"I can resist anything but temptation."

OSCAR WILDE

p. 172
. . . and then as if cloaked by moist blossoms
we stepped into the ancient wood of myth.

Stefan George: *The Year of the Soul*

p. 175.
Ding an sich, the thing per se, according to Kant, the thing
as existing independently of a perceiving subject, "true"
being, whose "appearances" or "manifestations" are the
empirical things to which the "phenomena" point.